Foreword

To Share in the Life of Christ

Experiencing God in Everyday Life

Laurence L. Gooley, S.J.

Saint Louis
The Institute of Jesuit Sources
1997

Number 18 in Series IV:
Studies on Jesuit Topics

Library of Congress Card Number 97-74246
ISBN 1-880810-27-1

This book is a revised version of *Experiencing God in Everyday
Life*, privately published by the author in 1993 and revised by
him in 1996.

Contents

Preface

Father Laurence Gooley has written a remarkable book, one that looks in two directions at once.

For every follower of Christ, there is a great deal in this slender volume to ponder and learn regarding prayer, community, commitment, service, and other themes basic to Catholic Christianity.

This broad perspective is, however, placed in a particular context, that of the Christian Life Communities. The book is a handbook for CLC which expertly guides its user from the very first CLC meeting that he or she attends to quite far along in the development of that user's spirituality as a member of that community. If such were all that the book is, its appeal would be limited to CLC members. That is not the case. A reader can readily extrapolate much of Fr. Gooley's material to fit the more widespread group of Christians who simply want to know, love, and serve the Lord.

Through this book, Fr. Gooley serves his fellow CLC members very well; but he serves the wider Church equally fruitfully.

John W. Padberg, S.J.
Director,
Institute of Jesuit Sources.

The Purpose of This Book

The experience of God is a journey of the heart. As Saint Ignatius says in his Spiritual Exercises, "It is not so much knowledge we seek as it is to taste and relish" what we seek. Good theology is of course fundamental to an adult relationship with God, but we do not reason our way into that relationship: we surrender ourselves into it.

This book is based on Ignatian spirituality. It offers a lived experience of the vision of Christian Life Community (CLC), and it also leads to a heightened awareness of personal interior movements inspired by the Spirit. Though written for members of CLC, this book can be equally fruitful for anyone desiring an experience of God. Whether individually or within community, let God be the guide in this journey of the heart.

How to Use This Book

It will sometimes happen that your prayer will not be in line with the theme of a particular exercise in the book. This of course is fine. You must always honor the prayer the Spirit places in your heart. This does not mean, however, that you will not still be using this book. It is not a matter of either using this book or following your own prayer; it is both. By that I mean each member prayerfully reads the selected exercise and then follows the prayer that is in her or his heart. In doing this, the community together enjoys the advantage of following a common theme while at the same time honoring the prayer of each individual. What is shared in the meetings is the fruit of both your reading of the exercise and your personal prayer.

This book is not a collection of lessons or essays to be read. Rather, what it contains is—like the Spiritual Exercises of Saint Ignatius—a set of spiritual exercises (aerobics, if you will) to be done. It is in their doing that they bear fruit.

Doing these exercises is not an end in itself: they are not a set of exercises to be gone through rigidly in the order presented. Rather, they are to be used in whatever way is helpful to the community, adapting even the format of the meeting to the needs of the community. So, for instance, when something in an exercise strikes you, do not hesitate to stop for a while and spend time with it. The exercises are not a set of literature assignments that must each be assimilated before you move on to the next one. Or, if one theme leads you to another one a good deal farther on in the book, follow that inspiration. It is true that these exercises do build upon one another, but they are still to be used in ways that prove most helpful. Finally, there is never the need to complete any given exercise.

The fruit of these exercises is not found in how well you did them, but rather in how deeply they affected you. Put another way, it is not the experience of these exercises that you are seeking but rather the experience of God while doing them. The more deeply you enter into them, the more you are opened to the experience of God. Given that each person's experience of God is unique, there is no expectation as to what anyone's experience in an exercise "should" be. Each person's experience is to be respected. Your sharing in your community is about your relationship with God in light of these exercises.

It follows from this that you need always be aware of what is happening in your heart when engaged in spiritual activity. We should always ask of an exercise, "What is my experience saying to me? What is happening in me? What is going on in me?" Being strongly inspired by an exercise, for instance, may mean that this aspect of spirituality is an area towards which the Spirit is moving you. Having difficulty with a particular exercise, however, may mean that you were too tired and distracted when you tried to do it. You may need to approach prayer at a more suitable time and place. Again, not doing an exercise at all may indicate that your life in general is too busy and unfocused. Whatever the experience you have, whether it be uplifting or difficult, the important thing is to ask, "What is this experience saying to me, and what response is it calling forth from me?" This is discernment. To this these exercises lead.

Finally, at the end of each exercise, the first question under "Reflection" asks how your presence to others and your experience of a particular exercise impact each other. This is meant to help you integrate your interior spiritual growth with how you are living out CLC's mission to be Christ for others.

Faith Sharing: Telling Your Story

Faith sharing, or "telling your story," reveals the action of God in your life and the quality of your response. The sharing is two-fold: it speaks to how you were touched by a particular exercise and how you responded in your prayer. Receiving one another's sharing without comment or question develops an environment of freedom and safety for members to share. The one doing the sharing can always ask for feedback. Above all, confidentiality must be respected.

Some obstacles that might interfere with faith sharing:
>—slipping into dialogue,
>—"head-tripping" into abstract thoughts,
>—forcing people to speak, or not accepting what is said,
>—talking too long, limiting time for others to share.

The Grace Prayed for, and the Grace Received

There is a two-fold movement throughout all the exercises in this book. The first of these is *the grace to be prayed for*, which is stated at the beginning of each exercise. In one case, this will be for "openness and surrender to God"; in another, "to know how God is calling me to care for others." This grace is specific: it is given, it is stated, it is what I am to desire and pray for throughout the exercise.

The second movement is *the grace received*, or what Saint Ignatius calls the "colloquy." This comes at the end of each exercise and has to do with how God touched me during this time. It is not stated in the exercise what this grace "should" be; rather, the exercise at this point stands back and lets the Spirit move the person and give what the Spirit will. This is a time of intimate sharing with God of the affective movements experienced during this exercise—of the "grace received from God."

We do not know in advance how we will be touched in our prayer. This is the mystery of spiritual growth: our prayer is guided by God's Spirit; what we pray for is guided by what we receive.

This interplay between *the grace I pray for* and *the grace I receive* is the dynamic within which spiritual growth happens. For instance, I may receive the grace I prayed for, such as becoming clear about a life vocation. On the other hand, I may find that I have not received the grace I prayed for, such as rejoicing with Jesus who is risen. Instead I become aware of a deep anger that has been residing in me for a long time. I reflect on what this is saying to me and return to prayer asking the Spirit to show me how to work through it. The gift of this *grace received* now guides what I pray for.

How we are touched by God may seem unexpected at times and unrelated to what we are praying for, but in faith we know that God totally loves us and will lead us to our truest and deepest selves. Our response can only be to be open to however God touches us; and when we are, it will suddenly dawn on us that we are in fact receiving precisely what our prayer is constantly searching for: openness and surrender to God.

This dynamic between *the grace I pray for* and *the grace I receive* is two-fold: I am intentional in what I pray for, which prevents following whim; and I am open to the grace I receive, which prevents rigid prayer. This interplay, which is at the heart of each exercise, facilitates the growing simplification of prayer and prepares the way for discernment.

Both graces can happen throughout the exercise, and they can even happen simultaneously. Consequently our prayer is to permeate the entire exercise; it is not something we do only at the beginning and the end of it. And our prayer is to be one that comes from the heart, from a hunger, a longing, a desire, so that when we pray for openness and surrender to God, for example, we do so with hope and expectation.

Thus, the heart of each exercise, and the dynamic for spiritual growth, is in this interplay between *the grace prayed for* and *the grace received*.

Acknowledgments

The author wishes to give special thanks to Sr. Sylvia Swanke, RSM, the co-developer of Christian Life Community Northwest, for her article on prayer, which is given in the Appendix. Her sharing of her own experience with CLC, along with her suggestions and critiques of the exercises in this handbook, were invaluable.

Grateful acknowledgement is also given to the formation team of CLC of English Canada for permission to adapt and revise much of its material from its *English Canadian Formation Manual I* for use in this book.

Format for Meetings

Check-in: with the group seated in a circle, each shares how each is feeling as the meeting begins. (10 minutes total)

Prayer: music, scripture, a reading, silence, anything that helps move the members into the spirit of the meeting. (5 minutes)

Read Aloud the entire exercise to be used for the meeting.

Sharing: may be around such questions as, "What struck me in this exercise? How was I moved by it during the last two weeks? How have I experienced God during this time?" Sharings are received in silence. All are free to ask for feedback on their own sharing at any time. When all are finished, members may be asked if there is anything they wish to add. Close with a prayer.

Break

Discussion: on anything that is affecting the life of the community.

Business: issues, place for next meeting, facilitator, etc.

Review of Meeting: each person reflects back to the group, "How was I moved during this meeting? Where did I feel positive energy, where did I feel discomfort?" What is surfaced here may become topics for discussion in future meetings.

Closing Prayer and Social.

Take and Receive

Take, Lord, and receive all my liberty,

My memory, my understanding,

And my entire will,

All I have and call my own.

You have given all to me.

To you, Lord, I return it.

Everything is yours; do with it what you will.

Give me only your love and your grace;

That is enough for me.

(—St. Ignatius of Loyola)

Soul of Christ

Jesus, may all that is you flow into me.

May your body and blood be my food and drink.

May your passion and death be my strength and life.

Jesus, with you by my side enough has been given.

May the shelter I seek be the shadow of your cross.

Let me not run from the love which you offer,

But hold me safe from the forces of evil.

On each of my dyings shed your light and your love.

Keep calling to me until that day comes

When, with your saints, I may praise you forever.

Amen.

*(—A favorite prayer of St. Ignatius,
as translated by David L. Fleming, S.J.*)*

---

* See Fr. Fleming's *The Spiritual Exercises of Saint Ignatius: a Literal Translation and a Contemporary Reading* (St. Louis: Institute of Jesuit Sources, 1991), p.3. A more recent translation can be found in Fr. Fleming's *Draw Me Into Your Friendship: A Literal Translation and a Contemporary Reading of the Spiritual Exercises* (St. Louis: Institute of Jesuit Sources, 1996), p.3.

Part One

Introduction to
Christian Life Community

One: The First Meeting

Check-in: with the group seated in a circle, give your name and briefly indicate how you are feeling as you begin this meeting.

Opening Prayer

Sharing Who We Are: You are beginning to explore Christian Life Community. You are invited to begin by sharing any three things about yourself, but including what brought you to CLC. After a few moments, whoever is ready may begin sharing. Please remember that this is a time in which we simply listen to one another without question or comment.

Discussion:
1) Comments or questions about the meeting format or anything else of concern about CLC.
2) Preview Exercises 2, 3, 4, and 5, recalling that the focus of the sixth meeting (Exercise 6) will be the decision whether to continue on in CLC.

Next Meeting: CLC is about mission, which begins to be considered on page 5. The focus for your prayer and reflection for next meeting will be on the following questions:
1) When have I experienced my relationship with God

flowing over into my relationship with others?
2) Where do I see poverty and injustice around me?
You may use the Scripture passages given on page 5 for your
prayer and reflection.

Review of the Evening: "How was I moved during this meeting?"

Two: Mission in CLC

With the help of the following scripture passages, pray for the grace to know if you are called to Christian Life Community:
- *Mt. 25:31-46 (the last judgment)*
- *Lk. 10:25-37 (the good Samaritan)*
- *Jn. 13:1-5 (washing of the feet)*

Mission is not so much something we do as it is the quality of our presence . . . to be Christ-bearers, like Mary. Christ's mission was not just what He did; it was who He was. His life and death revealed his Father's love. We reveal this love by seeking to build the sort of world in which people can live as sisters and brothers of a loving God. Anything that is about caring and loving is about mission.

The basis of mission is to be found in the truth that God is in all things. It is the same God in others who is in me. To love and serve God in myself is to love and serve God in others. It is the same God. When I do not work for peace and dignity for God's people, I do not love and in fact dishonor God in me.

The mission of CLC is to be Christ for others. This mission is best understood within our relationship with God. It is a gift of that relationship. As children are the gift of spousal love, mission is the gift of my relationship with God. As fire is to heat, CLC's mission is an outpouring of our relationship with God; and our relationship with God is expressed in our mission. They are one. Each completes the other. We would have to break our relationship with God not to be in mission. I don't choose mission; it chooses me. I don't find it; I receive it. It is not something to be solved; it is something to be thanked.

If anyone says, "My love is fixed on God" yet hates his brother, he is a liar. One who has no love for the brother he has seen cannot love the God he has not seen (1 Jn. 4:20) . . . If a brother has nothing to wear and no food for the day and you say to him, "Good bye and good luck! Keep warm and well fed!" but do not meet his bodily needs, what good is that? So it is with the faith that does nothing in practice. It is thoroughly lifeless (James 2:14-17).

Viewing mission as taking on one more project misses the point. Mission is not about project; it is misleading to speak of an individual's or a community's mission. There is only one mission for all CLC, and that is to love and serve God in all things.

The ways of living out this mission, however, are number-less. How we are guided is a very personal matter. It is at this point that discernment steps in. How we as individuals are called by God to this can be recognized through what we feel attracted to. That is the key—what we are attracted to, what we want to do, what we feel passionate about. Seen in this way, mission is liberating, it is energizing and fulfilling, because we are following our deepest desires which are God's desires for us. Mission reveals who we are and will lead us to greater personal fulfillment, freedom, and peace.

How a community might live out CLC's mission might be through the support of each member's efforts in this matter. The community can also call its members to be faithful to following their promptings from the Holy Spirit. It might also be that the community will engage in a common service, though the members need not all be doing the same thing in it. Mission in CLC is not a human initiative; it is the certainty of being sent as the disciples were sent by Jesus and Jesus was sent by his Father.

The gift of mission in CLC will manifest itself in:
- *revealing:* God's love for all people and creation;
- *bearing witness:* to Christ so as to establish his reign of justice and peace;
- *giving priority:* to the renewal and reform of society;
- *liberating:* victims from discrimination;
- *striving:* for a preferential option for the poor.

> *We are to become identified*
> *with his mission of bringing the good news to the poor,*
> *proclaiming liberty to captives and to the blind,*
> *new sight,*
> *setting the downtrodden free . . . .*
> *Our life is essentially apostolic.*
> From the "General Principles of Christian Life Community," article 8; see below, p. 119).

Reflection:
1) When have I experienced my relationship with God flowing over into my relationship with others?
2) Where do I see poverty and injustice around me?

Symbol: Find something of your own that reminds you of God's overwhelming love.

Grace Received: What struck you during this exercise? How were you moved?

Three: Spirituality of CLC

With the help of the following scriptures, pray for the grace to know if you are called to Christian Life Community:
- *Ps. 138 (a grateful heart)*
- *Mk. 1:16-20 (follow me)*
- *Mk. 8:27-30 (who do you say that I am?)*
- *Jn. 21:1-15 (Jesus appears at the lake)*

What makes CLC different from every other way of following Christ is that CLC is based on the Spiritual Exercises of St. Ignatius. Ignatian spirituality is a way of integrating the Gospel into one's daily life. It does not promote a particular style of response to it, nor outline a precise program of what to do. It describes the Gospel's call to join in Christ's universal mission to reveal his Father's love for all creation. It is a call to reinvent the Gospel for oneself, to discover anew what needs to be done to continue Christ's mission today.

The Spiritual Exercises, which describe Ignatius's own conversion, are the description of his spirituality. They are spiritual aerobics: not something to be read, but something to be worked through. They lead to a growing sensitivity to God's way of approaching and calling me. They guide one's travel with Jesus and how to meet him at the heart of the human adventure. They lead to discerned choices as to how to join in Christ's mission.

Other spiritual traditions have specific charisms for living out the Gospel. Franciscans, for instance, highlight simplicity and poverty, Benedictines community and hospitality, and Dominicans orthodoxy in doctrine and devotion to Mary. The Ignatian charism seeks the greater glory of God, its method is discernment, and its work is whatever promotes the greater good.

Ignatian spirituality is very practical; it aims to "get the job done." The mysticism of the Carmelites in John of the Cross has been described as contemplating the face of God in prayer. The mysticism of Ignatius in his Spiritual Exercises has been described as contemplating the face of God in the people whom we serve. This is the spirituality of CLC—having an authentic experience of God as we work with Jesus and one another for the salvation of all people and all creation.

What this calls for and leads to is spiritual freedom. Ignatius describes this interior openness and availability to God's invitations as "indifference." By this he does not mean "not caring one way or the other" about a path to be followed or a decision to be made. Of course there are prospects and possibilities about which we have feelings, some attracting us and others repelling us. The presence of feelings in fact is quite natural, and discerning them is encouraged. What Ignatius is getting at is that we keep ourselves "in balance" until we perceive how God is moving us, and then we follow.

Indifference—Spiritual Freedom—Keeping Ourselves in Balance: has to do with looking at our feelings and following those which lead to God. Spiritual freedom becomes active when our openness to God leads us past the paralysis of our fears and doubts into the joy and peace of being about the work of Jesus's Father. Spiritual freedom is felt when we have reached past our surface and sometimes intense feelings of reluctance and suspicion and embrace our deepest and truest desires, which are God's desires for us.

Living with the poor and sharing their condition,
Jesus invites all of us
to give ourselves continuously to God
and to bring about unity in our human family.
Inspired by the Holy Spirit,
we respond

with gratitude to God
for this gift of Jesus
in every circumstance of our lives.
(From *General Principles and General Norms*, 1.
See Appendix, p. 117, below.)

The spirituality of CLC, then, is:
   —*finding God in all things,*
   —*following the movements of the Spirit,*
   —*collaborating with Jesus,*
   —*ordering true relationships with Jesus and creation,*
   —*living in true interior freedom.*[*]

Reflection:
  1) Who is Christ for you?
  2) Where do you find Christ in your life today? What is
      your response to him?

Ritual Activity: Find a place where you feel the presence of Christ.

Grace Received: Where were you moved in this exercise? What has stayed with you?

---

[*] See *A Manual of Formation for Christian Life Community*, compiled by the Formation Team, CLC of English Canada (Guelph, Ontario: Office of English Canada CLC, 1989), pp. R43-44. Future references to this work will use the shorter title, *Canadian Manual*.

Four: Community in CLC

With the help of the following scriptures, pray for the grace to know if you are called to Christian Life Community:
- *Mt. 18:20 (where two or three are together)*
- *Lk. 10:1-21 (mission of the seventy-two)*
- *Jn. 15:1-10 (the vine and the branches)*
- *Acts 2:42-47 (communal life).*

Christian Life Community is a world-wide community composed of small groups of women and men who seek to unite their human life in all its dimensions with the fullness of Christian faith. These local communities are the face and expression of the World Community. They are communities of persons who are committed to one another. Through their prayer over scripture and their listening to others' experiences of God, they become at ease with one another, able to entrust care and reverence to one another, and to expend a Gospel quality of love that heals and reveals Christ to the world.

Being part of the World Community means that CLC is more than the local community. The charism of CLC is "living in community," whoever the members of a local group may be. CLC is about having a communitarian relationship with God.

This in no way lessens the value and beauty of the local community's life together. Its bonds of support and love are pure gift. Being part of a larger community simply enhances that experience, for it widens the focus of the community to include a world view that is in harmony with the world-wide mission of CLC. In fact, since the mission of CLC is to be Christ in the world, the community of CLC can only be world-wide.

The community is a place of apostolic discernment. It is where members come to seek from one another support and even guidance in discerning their life choices. By being present to one another in this way, the members actually take on the religious commitments of one another as part of their own. The community, in other words, becomes the ordinary way of discovering how best to be Christ in our modern world.

This is why community in CLC is more than a support group. It does not exist for its own sake. It is what energizes us to go back out into life and follow Christ's invitation to work with him in his work of love for peace. It is the place we go out from to share a Christ-like quality of presence to others, and the place we return to for nourishment. The community not only helps us discern the Spirit's movements within us, it also calls us to be faithful to the Spirit's call.

There is no one type of community in CLC. The shape of each grows out of the experience of the care and concern its members show for one another and the world. The community is in service to CLC's mission to be Christ for others and is in turn shaped by it. The love and support that one woman received from her community, for instance, led her to commit to making her whole life a witness to Christ's love for us. A young man's experience in working for two weeks in a summer camp for disabled children profoundly affected his experience of his CLC community. CLC is a Christian way of life; it is a vocation.

Reflection:
1) What has been your experience of community?
2) What has been your experience of Christian community?

Ritual Activity: Go into a church or public area and view the people as members in Christ's community of love.

Grace Received: What struck you in this exercise? What attracted you? What did not attract you?

> *We live this way of Christian life*
> *in joyful communion with all those who have preceded us,*
> *grateful for their efforts and apostolic accomplishments.*
> *In love and prayer we join*
> *those many men and women of our spiritual tradition*
> *who have been proposed to us by the Church*
> *as friends and valid intercessors*
> *who help us to fulfill our mission.*
>
> (From *General Principles*, #3.
> See below, page 117f.)

Five: Being Christ for Others

With the following scriptures, pray for the grace to hear how God is calling you to live for others. (See above, page xii f.)
- *Mt. 25:31-46 (the last judgment)*
- *Lk. 10:25-37 (the good Samaritan)*
- *Jn. 13:1-15 (washing of the feet).*

Christian Life Community is a world community of Christian women and men who seek to know, love, and serve God in all persons and in all situations. With Christ, CLC endeavors to promote the value of the Gospel which affects the dignity of the person, the welfare of the family, and the integrity of creation. Like Christ, it seeks to communicate God's compassionate message of liberation to those who so desperately need it, especially the poor and victims of oppression. As individuals, members encourage and support one another in this effort. As community, they seek to draw others toward this same unity of life.

CLC does not prescribe how to do this. Rather, it assists members, through the charism of Ignatian spirituality, to discern how each feels called, through what attracts him or her, to be Christ for others. CLC is guided not by a set of rules but by the spirit of the Gospel and the interior law of love. This law of love, which the Spirit inscribes in our hearts, expresses itself anew in each new situation of our daily lives. This Spirit-inspired love respects the uniqueness of each personal vocation and enables members to be open and free, always at the disposal of God in seeking a world of justice and peace.

The mission of CLC is not so much something that we do as it is a quality of presence, the presence of Jesus himself. His mission was not just what He did; it was who He was, his whole life. CLC mission is to carry on Christ's mission of being people who reveal God's love. They not only do this—they are which people can live together as sisters and brothers and as daughters and sons of God. The conversion of hearts for justice and peace announces the Reign of God.

The heart of CLC mission is in being open to Christ's Spirit, in embracing God's saving love in every moment of life. From the ordinary routine of everyday life to choices made in the service of others, all human activity becomes part of this mission when it is grounded in love. The field of CLC knows no limits. CLC is more than a prayer group; it is a way of life. CLC mission is all around us. All we need to do is embrace it.

Reflection:

1) How do you see yourself living for others? Do you see it as a ministry?

2) Using the scriptures above, pray for the grace to learn how God is attracting you to live for others.

Ritual Activity: Several times during the next two weeks, sit quietly and let the gift of your living for others touch your heart.

Grace Received: What struck you from this exercise? How did God touch you through this experience? Was it difficult? Was it uplifting? What was the grace you received? This will be the focus of your faith sharing at the next meeting. (See pages xii f., above.)

Six: Am I Called to CLC?

With the help of the following scriptures, pray for the grace to know whether God is calling you to CLC (see pp. xii f., above).
- *Jn. 14:1-18 (have faith in God)*
- *Mt. 11:25-30 (come to me)*
- *Jer. 29:11-14 (I have plans for you)*
- *1 Sam. 3:1-10 (here I am, Lord).*

We have begun forming a CLC community. In our meetings we have tried to be open to ourselves, to one another, and to God. We began addressing the questions, "What is the use of my life? What gives value to my life? How do my life, work, relationships, and leisure escape insignificance? What am I searching for?" We began looking at life as St. Ignatius did: trying to find God in all things.

The question now is, "Do I feel called to continue exploring CLC?"

We have seen that CLC involves:

—commitment to prayer: a regular practice of prayer according to each one's way;

—commitment to one another through regular attendance at meetings;

—growth in one's relationship with God through sharing and reflection on Ignatian spirituality;

—the desire to be about something, that my life be of service to my sisters and brothers.

It is not the idea that all of this be accomplished before we can commit ourselves to CLC. These are rather ideals that we continually seek, and even desiring them places us within the spirit of what CLC is about.

The following questions may be helpful as you discern whether you feel called to continue exploring CLC, or whether you feel called to look for God in another way.

- ◆ What am I looking for spiritually?
- ◆ Does CLC help meet these needs?
- ◆ Does the experience of Ignatian spirituality help me understand my inner experiences?
- ◆ Do I desire to grow in the direction that CLC offers?

Reflection:
1) Using the scriptures provided, pray for the grace to know if God is calling you to CLC.
2) During the next meeting's faith sharing, you will be invited to share your decision regarding CLC.
3) For those continuing in CLC, preview the exercise on page 21, below, for the next meeting.

Activity: Pray during the next two weeks all the "Graces To Be Prayed For" from the first six meetings. Then, just before the next meeting, write out in your own words how you feel the Spirit is guiding you regarding CLC.

Grace Received: What have been the gifts for you during these first six meetings? How have you been blessed? (See pp. xii f., above.)

Because our Community is a way of Christian life,
these [general] principles are to be interpreted
not so much by the letter of this text
as by the spirit of the Gospel and the interior law of love.
This law of love, which the Spirit inscribes in our hearts,
expresses itself anew in each situation of our daily lives.
This Spirit-inspired love
respects the uniqueness of each personal vocation
and enables us to be open and free,
always at the disposal of God.
It challenges us to see our responsibilities

and constantly to seek answers to the needs of our times,
to work together with the entire People of God
and all people of good will
to seek progress and peace,
justice and charity,
liberty and dignity for all.

(From *General Principles*, #2.
See below, page 117.)

Part Two

Experiencing Prayer

Seven: The Consciousness Examen

With the help of the following scriptures, pray for the grace to be sensitive to how God touches you.
- *Rom. 16:25-27 (doxology)*
- *Col. 1:25-29 (the mystery: Christ in us)*
- *Col. 3:12-15 (practice of virtues)*
- *Jn. 15:9-17 (love as I have loved you).*

The Consciousness Examen is sometimes called the Discernment Examen or an Awareness Review. By whatever name, the Examen is a simple prayer exercise that makes us more aware of our inner movements—feelings, motives, and inspirations—that deepen and order our lives to God. Looking at these movements makes us more attuned to the inspirations of the Holy Spirit and more alert to the promptings of evil.

This examen—the one prayer that Saint Ignatius insisted that his men never omit—is *the* prayer exercise in Ignatian spirituality. Since it is a discernment reflection, it is the prayer of CLC. Of all the prayer and reflections offered in this handbook, this is the one to keep doing: in season and out, in noisy places and in quiet, during the day and during the night, in good times and in hard times (especially in hard times). It is to be done always, because it strengthens our awareness of God's awareness of us.

The Consciousness Examen is not about good or bad actions, but about how God is moving me. Its focus is not on me, it is on God *in* me; it is not about how well or poorly I do, it is about how generously I respond to God's loving me. The goal of the examen is to develop a heart with a discerning vision, which will be active not only during examens, but continually in my life, a gift to be prayed for. Finding God in all things for Ignatius was what life was all about. My life is no longer an "I," but rather a "we."

The Examen is quite simple and natural. It can be done twice a day, once a day, once every few days—however often a person feels moved to do it with the greatest fruit. The more we do it, the more natural it becomes for us, and it eventually becomes a way of consciousness, a way of being in ever-closer relationship with God. Performing it can take anywhere between five and fifteen minutes. It doesn't really matter how long you spend; the important thing is that you open yourself up to recognizing and responding to God's movements in you. However, it is better not to go longer than fifteen minutes; anything beyond this time begins to move the Examen's focus away from being a review of our relationship with God during a period of time.

Saint Ignatius suggests five steps to the Examen. Before looking at those, however, it is well to realize that eventually one needs to structure the examen in a way that is most helpful and natural for each given person. There is no one right way to do it; nor is there a need to go through all of Saint Ignatius's five points each time. You might, for instance, find yourself spending time on the first point at one time, and on the fifth point at some other time. Go to wherever you are drawn.

Saint Ignatius's five points are as follows:

♦ *Prayer for Light:* I am before God who loves me and welcomes me, who enlightens me and guides me. I embrace God who lives and grows in me.

♦ *Gratitude:* I give thanks for what I have done and for what I have received this day, both pleasant and difficult, for the word of encouragement and the generous gesture, for my family and work, my community, for the time to pray and to laugh and to cry.

♦ *Review of the Day:*

—What has happened to me in my life, my work, my relationships? How has God been working in me? What has been asked of me?

—What has been the quality of my response: with love

or selfishness, with honesty or deceit?

♦ *Ask for Forgiveness:* I ask pardon for when I refused to understand my sisters and brothers in their pain, for passing up the opportunity to be useful, for my failure in loving, for injustices, for oppression. I ask pardon for not loving God and all creation in every part of my life.

♦ *Hopeful Recommitment:* I seek to respond and trust God, aware of my weakness but confident in God's strength and mercy. I want to flourish for my sisters and brothers. I renew my commitment to follow the path that God offers me to be a source of light for all creation. Saint Ignatius suggests ending with an *Our Father*.[*]

Reflection: How has the Examen helped me see God in my life?

Symbol: Find something that expresses reconciliation and closeness to God.

Grace Received: How has God touched you in this exercise? How were you moved? This will be the focus of your next meeting's faith-sharing.

> *Through the daily faith-consciousness examen*
> *and through personal and communal discernment,*
> *we try to give an apostolic sense*
> *to even the most humble realities of daily life.*
> —General Principles, #8b.

---

[*] For a complete treatment of the Consciousness Examen, see *Canadian Manual,* pp. R95-101.

Eight: Praying for a Grace

With the help of the following scriptures, pray for the grace of openness and surrender to God in prayer.
- *Ex. 17:8-13 (Moses kept his arms raised)*
- *Ps. 62:2 (only in God is my soul at rest)*
- *Jer. 20:7-9 (the word of the Lord burns my heart)*
- *Lk. 7:36-50 (she has not ceased kissing my feet)*
- *Lk. 11:5-13 (ask and you shall receive).*

Saint Ignatius emphasizes in his Spiritual Exercises that we are to pray for that which we desire, to taste and relish the grace for which we pray. At one time this is "to ask for the gift of a growing and intense sorrow for my sins"; at another time, "to ask for the grace to know Jesus intimately, to love him more intensely, and so to follow him more closely"; still again, it is "to ask for the grace to enter into the joy and consolation of Jesus in the victory of his risen life."

Praying for a grace is a matter of the heart, of longing, of hunger, of desire; it is praying with emotion. There is no place for polite, appropriate, or reserved prayer. We pray with insistence over and over again.

Good models for this are the Psalmists and Jeremiah, who poured out their feelings and needs to Yahweh. They knew that God was the One who could take it, and would understand. Listen to the exuberant joy pouring out in Ps. 148, 1ff.:

Praise Yahweh from the heavens, praise Yahweh in the heights; praise Yahweh, all you angels; praise Yahweh, all you hosts! Praise Yahweh, sun and moon; praise Yahweh, all you shining stars! Praise Yahweh, you highest heavens, and you waters above the heavens!

Or listen to Jeremiah as he laments the call given him by Yahweh in chapter 20:7ff.:

You duped me, O Yahweh, and I let myself be duped; you were too strong for me and you triumphed. . . .

Cursed be the day on which I was born! May the day my mother gave me birth never be blessed! Cursed be the man who brought the news to my father, saying, "A child, a son, has been born to you!" . . . Then my mother would have been my grave, her womb confining me forever. Why did I come forth from the womb, to see sorrow and pain, to end my days in shame? . . . I say to myself, I will not mention Yahweh's name, I will speak his name no more. But then it becomes like fire in my heart, imprisoned in my bones; I grow weary holding it in, I cannot endure it.

This is passion and total vulnerability before God—beautiful! They are a far cry from the rote, repetitious, and monotonous prayers that we hear and so often say ourselves. The invitation here is to throw ourselves into prayer with complete abandon and trust, like a child who without any hesitation or fear crawls into the lap of a loving mother or father.

As you pray for the grace in this and succeeding exercises, do so frequently: at the beginning, throughout the middle, and at the end of each exercise, and in between as well, doing so with energy and expectation. To pray in this manner is to acknowledge that growth in prayer is God's gift and not our work. It puts us in the position of receiver rather than doer.

When we pray for a grace, we leave part of our being open to receive it; I make a certain area of my life available for God's action. And, as I pray frequently for a grace, I find that a general grace becomes more particular according to my needs. For example, I may be praying for the awareness of how my Creator relates to me personally, and towards the middle of the week I discover that I am afraid of letting others relate personally to me. So I begin to pray for the trust I need. Praying for a grace gets us in touch with our deepest desires. It becomes a process of self-discovery.

Saint Ignatius goes on to say that if we don't desire a particular grace, then we should pray to desire it. Again, the prayer comes out of the heart: desired, felt, and hungered for.

Such prayer helps inspire and make real to us that for which we pray; it develops our inner freedom to be open to the gift of the grace.[*]

Reflection:
   1) How does living for others affect your experience of praying for a grace?
   2) Do you truly desire and hunger for the grace above?
   3) Recall that if you do not desire a grace, you are to pray to desire it.
   4) Using the scriptures given above, pray repeatedly and with longing to surrender yourself to God.

Gesture: Do body movements and gestures that express for you the grace you received. (See below, p. 112.)

Grace Received: What struck you during the past two weeks? What was revealed to you?

We hold the Spiritual Exercises of Saint Ignatius as the specific source and the characteristic instrument of our spirituality. Our vocation calls us to live this spirituality, which opens and disposes us to whatever God wishes in each concrete situation of our daily life. We recognize particularly the necessity of prayer and discernment, personal and communal, of the daily examination of consciousness and of spiritual guidance as important means for seeking and finding God in all things.
                                    —General Principles, #4.
                                    (See below, p. 118.)

---

[*] See *Canadian Manual*, p. R69.

Nine: Praying with Scripture

With the help of the following scriptures, pray for the grace of openness and surrender to God in prayer.
- *Rom. 8:26-27 (the Spirit helps in our weakness)*
- *1 Cor. 12:12-26 (we are one body)*
- *Is. 55:10-11 (Yahweh cannot fail)*
- *Lk. 24:13-33 (road to Emmaus)*
- *Lk. 7:36-50 (the woman wiped Jesus's feet).*

This is an exercise about developing the relationship between scripture and prayer. Now, God is continually reaching out to us and inviting us to respond, continually speaking to us and inviting us to listen. How do we go about listening? In the case of other people, we hear words and thoughts directly. With God, however, we become aware of the divine presence, of being open to this presence. Finding a quiet place helps to do this. When we relax and let go of our concerns and anxieties, our projects and worries, we become aware, we are entering into prayer.

Praying with scripture is a specially graced way of listening to God, of becoming aware of God's presence. There is a power in scripture that goes to the heart. Praying with scripture opens us to its saving power. It is, indeed, the preferred prayer in the Spiritual Exercises. Since they deal with becoming companions with Jesus, the biblical words leading up to and about Him are integral to our coming to know Him.

Praying with scripture is quite simple and natural, and there are many ways in which to do so. The five steps below suggest one way. But, like the steps outlined for the Consciousness Examen earlier, these steps are simply a suggestion: a good one, but not one meant to be followed rigidly. They are meant to be used and adapted according to your experience and the inspirations of the Holy Spirit.

Praying with Scripture: the Five "P's":

- ◆ *Passage:* Select a passage that you feel moved to spend time with.
- ◆ *Place:* Choose a place that is conducive to becoming quiet and calm and free.
- ◆ *Posture:* Become relaxed and peaceful — in a harmony of body and spirit.
- ◆ *Presence:* Be aware of the presence of God; acknowledge it and open your heart to it.
- ◆ *Passage:* Read the passage slowly and with care, aloud or in a whisper, in rhythm with your breathing, or by phrase and word. There is no need to finish the passage.

There is a saying: stop when something happens in prayer, when something strikes you in prayer. What does this mean? At certain points during prayer, there may be an inner movement, signaling a new way of being with Jesus or of experiencing God's love. It may be a feeling of being lifted up, of peace and contentment; or it may be a feeling of unease, unsettledness, even boredom. Whatever it is, pay attention when something strikes you, and spend time with those feelings to see what they are saying. A communication is happening. Later, when the prayer exercise is finished, thank God for loving and being faithful to you, and pray to receive the grace given.*

You may, in fact, find yourself stopping at any one of these five "P's": you might, for instance, find yourself spending much of your prayer in "Posture" or "Presence." Follow the Spirit! Whatever happens is good, and you should follow your own process for praying with scripture. Experiment! The best prayer for you is the prayer that works best for you. And do so in a relaxed, calm, and trustful way. The desire to be with

---

* See *Canadian Manual,* pp. R58-60.

God is enough; there is no need to prove, achieve, or accomplish anything in particular, and feeling that we have to do so is a deception. In prayer we are the patients, the receivers, and God is the giver. We simply open our hearts and love God, no matter how the prayer effort goes. Prayer is a grace; praying with scripture is a gift that we receive.

There may be some who are not very familiar with scripture, or accustomed to using it in prayer. It may take some time and experience for them to become used to it. Fine; there are no deadlines here, and no pressure to achieve. Rather, our focus is on loving God, letting God inspire and inform our prayer. Enter into the experience with openness and without anxiety. This is not a puzzle to be solved; it is a gift. God is found in our efforts to pray with scripture. Like the joy of watching a baby learn to walk, God's love surrounds our most earnest and oftentimes feeble efforts. Our effort is on loving God, allowing God to grace us.

Reflection:
   1) How has your care for others impacted your experience of this exercise?
   2) Never feel constrained to blot out all distractions. Anxiety gets between you and God. God can speak to you even in noise and confusion. Pray into the distractions, and they too become prayer.
   3) God is with you even in your seeming inability to pray. A humbled attitude of trying to pray, even when it seems impossible, is a sign of love for God, true prayer.
   4) Using the scriptures given above, pray for openness to God.

Activity: Spend some time reading scripture as a way of enhancing your experience of this exercise. (See below, p. 111f.)

Grace Received: What struck you during the past two weeks about this exercise? What was God trying to say to you? What was the grace you received?

Ten: Review of Prayer

With the help of the following scriptures, pray for the grace of a growth in confidence and trust in God's love for you.
- *Ps. 23 (Yahweh refreshes my soul)*
- *Mt. 14:23 (Jesus went off by himself to pray)*
- *Lk. 2:51 (Mary pondered these things in her heart)*
- *Lk. 9:28-36 (Lord, it is good for us to be here)*
- *Heb. 3:15 (hear; harden not your hearts).*

The Review of Prayer helps us notice what interior movements we felt during it. It enables us to be spontaneous during prayer and to "go with the flow" of what is happening. Monitoring ourselves during prayer interferes with God's communication. Rather, we let happen what is happening, and then, later, we look back to see what God was saying to us.

The Review is done after the prayer period is over. Its point is to recognize how God touched us in prayer, a touch that may have been accompanied by feelings of consolation, presence, hope, inspiration—or desolation, fear, anxiety, boredom, and so on. Each set of feelings reveals a different set of signals and meanings, and it is the work of discernment to identify which movements and feelings lead us towards God and which lead away from God. We even look at our distractions, especially if they were disturbing. We then reflect on what these various movements mean.

Questions like the following may help:
- ◆ What went on during the prayer?
- ◆ What struck me?
- ◆ How did I feel about what went on?
- ◆ What did God's Spirit show me?
- ◆ Is there some point that I should return to in my next prayer?

During this time I thank God for graces granted, and ask pardon for my negligence.

Even though in the Review there is some reflection on the

process and timing of our prayer, the Review is not about seeing how well we did. Prayer is not something to be achieved; it is something that we receive, a gift. And so the Review concentrates on how we were moved during prayer, what we felt, what were the affective movements going on in us. We exclude nothing from these movements, for even feelings of boredom, distractions, dryness, and even resistance are vehicles of God's communication and presence to us. What we feel helps make clear what God is trying to reveal to us.

For example: suppose that in my Review, I noticed resistance as I listened to Peter say at the Transfiguration, "Lord, it is good that we are here." I felt myself holding back from this, not wanting to get too close or open to Jesus. This may indicate a fear of getting too close to others, a poor self-image; it may follow from the memory of my parents not being close to me. This is a wonderful insight. God may be using this resistance to help me work through my fears, unresolved issues, or unhealed memories so as to become healed and free.

The Review keeps our prayer from remaining at surface level; it guides us in a process of self-discovery through our relationship with God. Develop whatever process you find helpful to review your prayer experience with God. This, with the Consciousness Examen, is another method of discernment.

It is often helpful to journal during the Review as a preparation for the next prayer. God may be extending the invitation to go back to a point where something was felt. Saint Ignatius says, "I should remain quietly meditating upon a point until I have been satisfied," that is, until the movement has been completed, the insight completed, the struggle resolved, the consolation ended, the meaningfulness finished — for now.*

---

* See *Canadian Manual*, p. R72.

Reflection:
1) How have your reaching out to others and your experience of this exercise impacted each other?
2) It is good to pause a while after your prayer and change positions before beginning the Review of Prayer. During the Review, note the feelings you had during the prayer.
3) Jot down these movements in a journal and use them for your next prayer. You may also use this journal with your spiritual director.
4) Using the scriptures above, continually pray for the grace above.

Symbol: Read something that is significant to you (poetry, a letter, and so on) and that symbolizes the grace you received from this exercise.

Grace Received: What has God shown you during this time? What have you come to realize? How have you been changed? This will be the focus of your faith-sharing at the next meeting.

Union with Christ leads us to union with the Church,
where Christ here and now continues his mission of salvation.
By making ourselves sensitive
to the signs of the times and the movements of the Spirit,
we will be better able to encounter Christ
in all persons and in all situations.
—General Principles, #6.
(See below, p. 118f.)

Eleven: Ignatian Contemplation

With the help of the following scriptures, pray for the grace to know, love, and follow Jesus more closely.
- *Jn. 8:1-11 (the woman caught in adultery)*
- *Mt. 14:22-33 (Jesus walks on the water)*
- *Lk. 5:1-11 (Jesus calls his disciples)*
- *Mk. 14:66-72 (Peter's denial of Jesus).*

Contemplation is the fundamental prayer of the Spiritual Exercises. But it is not a type of prayer that seeks solutions to questions or problems, nor is it a little imaginary play that portrays Jesus in new and novel ways. Contemplation is being present to the mystery of an event and to its meaning for me. We do not follow our own temperament, imagination, and feelings in encountering Christ; rather, the focus is on the mystery: we allow the scene to produce its effects in the depths of our hearts. Contemplation becomes the privileged means of encountering Christ in me, in my work, in people, and in the world.

Ignatian contemplation is a work of the heart. "It is not much knowledge that we seek," Ignatius states in his *Spiritual Exercises*; it is to "taste and relish" that which we contemplate. We are speaking of heart knowledge which is real and felt, not notional knowledge which is about the world of ideas. Knowledge and understanding are, to be sure, helpful and even crucial in having a mature relationship with God; but they are also at the service of the affections, of the heart. Prayer is not an exercise about God, but rather an experience of God.

Ignatian contemplation is about falling more deeply in love with God. It is a "looking long" at Jesus in the Gospels: his words, his actions, his attitudes, his way of being, the quality of his presence. It is letting the beauty, the truth, the mystery of his person and personality sink deeply into our hearts. And when they do so we are affected, we are changed, we are transformed and lifted to his level of beauty and truth: in other words, we have fallen more deeply in love with Jesus.

The process of Ignatian contemplation is very simple and natural; and it lends itself easily to adaptation according to our own disposition and temperament. Becoming acquainted and comfortable with this style of prayer may take a while, depending on each one's background and experience. But that should cause no one any anxiety. No one is ever at a disadvantage with God. There is no place for comparing the quality of my prayer with that of another. The important thing is growth in my relationship with God. Contemplation is one method that offers growth; and all of us have the capacity for a deeper, more intimate relationship with God.

Relax, then. Pray for help. Find the time and place for quiet, and let the experience of those whom you are contemplating in the Gospel teach you and somehow become your own experience.

The points given below offer some suggestions as to what might strike you if you were going to contemplate the passage of the woman caught in adultery in John 8:1-11. These suggestions, however, are merely possibilities; they are not meant to be gone through step by step *during* your prayer. So, read prayerfully through them, and then put them aside. Ask the Spirit to guide you. In your prayer, be present to what strikes you and to what you are feeling.

You could even try this contemplation now, during your meeting. Have someone read the passage from St. John slowly. You may feel confusion like the woman, or fear like the crowd, or compassion like Jesus. Whenever something strikes you, stay with it and let your interior movements speak to you. Whether consoling or unsettling, simply be present to them. Your contemplation is happening. Later you can look back to see what it is saying to you. Let the Spirit guide you.

- ♦ Close your eyes and relax. Breathe deeply, and become quiet for a time.

♦ Listen to the story of the woman caught in adultery.
♦ Be in the scene; watch it unfold. What do you see? hear? smell? feel?
♦ Watch the Scribes and Pharisees drag the woman with scorn before Jesus.
♦ Watch the crowd; feel their fear of the accusers. They watch Jesus.
♦ Watch the woman pushed into Jesus's presence, cowering in fear and shame, not looking up.
♦ Watch Jesus, drawing in the dust, weary of the Jewish leaders. His voice is soft and unafraid.
♦ Watch the leaders, trapped, embarrassed, and angry; they begin to leave.
♦ Watch the woman straighten up and turn to Jesus with amazement, gratitude, and relief.
♦ Now: where are you? in the crowd? with the Scribes and Pharisees? with the woman? with Jesus?
♦ Jesus looks up at you and says, " . . . " Spend time here. Let him touch your heart; be present to his truth for you. Your contemplation is beginning.
♦ When finished, slowly come back to the present. Thank Jesus for inviting you to be there.
♦ Do a "Review of Prayer." What did you feel during the prayer? What happened to you?*

---

* A summary description of Ignatian contemplation is given in John C. Futrell, S.J., and Marian Cowan, C.S.J., *The Spiritual Exercises of Saint Ignatius* (New York: LeJacq Publishing, Inc., 1982, pp. 83-86). This summary is reproduced below.

Contemplation of Jesus is the essential means to accomplish the renewal of faith that enables me to hear and discern the word of God at all times and to encounter Christ in people, in my work, and in the world (p. 83).

Contemplation is being present not just to the event, but to the meaning and mystery of that event and to its meaning and presence in my life now. It is not a little imaginary play, but "presence in faith" to a past event in order to let God penetrate and transform me (pp. 85-86).

Reflection:
1) Do your concerns for others and your contemplations influence one another?
2) Try doing this with a trusted friend, hearing the story told aloud.
3) Do not look for success. Contemplation is a grace to be prayed for, a gift to be received. Be patient.
4) Using the scriptures, pray to know, love, and follow Jesus more closely.

Each in contemplation must follow one's own temperament, imagination, and feelings which will then lead to a transforming encounter in faith with Jesus Christ. The Spiritual Exercises are a privileged time for discovering one's own best method of prayer here and now, perhaps even revising the method from what it has been up to now (p. 85).

Contemplation does not bring the Gospel down to one's own level; it lifts one by the Spirit to the level of the Gospel. Ignatius calls us to look long at Jesus — his words, actions, his interior attitudes, his way of being. Looking long lets the mystery penetrate to the depths of the heart and transform one in Christ (pp. 85-86).

One should avoid seeking applications in life too quickly. The light of the Spirit comes as gradual enlightenment. One should draw everything possible from the present contemplation, taking note of both consolations and desolations, seeing whether the Spirit takes them up later. Contemplation is a real purification of imagination and of understanding, a passing over entirely to the level of faith through the intense looking long at the mysteries of Jesus Christ (p. 86).

Activity: Do a "Mantra": a word or short phrase that is repeated frequently as a prayer. For instance, "Jesus," or "Jesus, have mercy on me," or a word or phrase of your own choosing.

Grace Received: What is God saying to you through your experience of this exercise? What invitation is God offering? What grace has been given you?

Twelve: Images of God

With the help of the following scriptures, pray for the grace of deep confidence and trust in God's personal care and love for you.
- *Mt. 19:13-15 (Jesus blesses the children)*
- *Lk. 15:11-32 (the prodigal child)*
- *Lk. 7:36-50 (the penitent woman)*
- *Mt. 8:5-13 (the centurion's servant)*
- *Jn. 8:2-11 (the woman caught in adultery).*

Intimacy is a basic issue in our relationship with God. We want to experience God's deep love and concern for us. Our fear is that this love and concern is not there. Our desire for this intimacy may be hidden in such vague hopes and desires as, "I want to get back to prayer"; "I need to re-charge the old spiritual batteries"; "I want to pray about a decision I have to make"; "I want to be alone with God for a while." There may well be truth in these wishes, but a deeper underlying truth is likely to be the desire for an intimate experience of God's loving me and caring for me.

A barrier to this experience is often the doubt that God does love and care for me in a personal way; it is a fear that God will not become present to me when I ask for this, that God cannot be bothered with the likes of me. These doubts and fears stem from our images and attitudes towards God. We imagine God, for instance, to be too distant and almighty even to be aware of me, let alone care for me. There are many images of God. For instance:

- ◆ God is the ultimate police officer.
  I must obey "the rules" or God will punish me. My life is one of fear.
- ◆ God protects the innocent and punishes the guilty.
  I must be guilty when something bad happens to me.

- God helps those who help themselves.
  The "unfortunates" don't deserve our compassion or our help.
- God's relationship with me is strictly a private thing.
  I have no responsibility to care for others.
- God's acceptance of me is proven through my successes.
  Failure means God has rejected me.
- God's will for me is some grand design into which I must fit my life.
  How I feel is not important in my relationship with God.
- God loves only those who are good.
  I am a bad person when I fail.
- God will always give what we ask if we pray hard enough.
  I have a crisis of faith when my prayers "are not answered" in the way I wanted.
- God loves me and wills to save me just as I am.
  I know I am loved and cared for no matter how well or how poorly I do.[*]

Our images of others sometimes do funny things to us, and that includes our images of God. Very often they are projections of how we see and feel about things. When we are fearful about something, we can picture God as one to fear. If we are prone to feelings of guilt, we can imagine God as intolerant of failure. If we were gifted with loving parents, we can see God as loving and caring. . . . And the list goes on. In other words, how we feel about ourselves often influences how we feel about God, and how we see God often reflects how we see ourselves.

---

[*] See the article entitled, "On Asking God to Reveal Himself in Retreat," by William A. Barry, S.J., in David L. Fleming, S.J. (ed.), *Notes on the Spiritual Exercises of St. Ignatius of Loyola* (St. Louis: Review for Religious, 1985), pp. 72-74.

Another aspect to this is that we can go through our whole lives having basically one image of God, reflecting probably a perception and experience of God from childhood. We can easily become trapped in such a perception of God even without realizing it. But our relationship with God that stems from that perception can be a very restricted one.

It is quite natural that our image of God is greatly influenced by the circumstances and events of our lives, but our experiences alone do not reveal much about God. True imaging of God does not come from us. It comes to us. It is a gift, the grace of a revelation. It is God who makes self-revelation to us most clearly in the revealed Word. The eyes of flesh and blood do not reveal much; God is most clearly seen with the eyes of faith.

Does that mean that there is only one true image of God? No. Our images come from different ways of experiencing God, which are limitless. This is why a maturing relationship with God moves through different images.

These images are not so much ones we come up with on our own, but rather ones that come to us, are given to us, are revealed to us through our experience of life and especially of scripture. The ongoing integration of our images with those revealed to us reflect the spiritual identity that is taking shape within us.

Reflection:
1) How does your image of God reflect your outreach to others?
2) What were your images of God when you were a child? What are they now? What would you like them to be?
3) What images of Jesus can you find in the Gospels?
4) Using the scriptures given above, pray for a deep trust and confidence in God's care and love for you.

Symbol: Choose something—a rock, a candle, a picture—that symbolizes what struck you in this exercise. Make it a part of your life these next two weeks. (See below, pp. 112ff.)

Grace Received: Have you received the grace you prayed for above? Do you desire to receive it?

Thirteen: Repetition of Prayer

With the help of the following scriptures, pray for the grace to trust in God's personal love and care for you (see Foreword, pp. xii f.).

- *Eph. 3:14-21 (may Christ dwell in your hearts)*
- *1 Jn. 4:7-19 (God dwells in us)*
- *Mt. 5:13-16 (you are the salt of the earth)*
- *Jn. 14:9b-21 (the Spirit of truth will be in you)*
- *Jer. 31:31-34 (I place my law in their hearts).*

"Repetition of Prayer" picks up where the Review of Prayer leaves off by returning to those points in an earlier prayer in which I experienced something—"greater consolation or desolation," in Saint Ignatius's terms, or even dryness. If those same feelings come back, then I need to spend more time with them in prayer to see what God is trying to communicate to me. If they don't come back, then I move on to my next prayer. This process deepens me and keeps me from remaining superficial in my prayer. Repetition of Prayer sharpens my sensitivity to God and is an important means of becoming open to God.

But there is a difference between Repetition of Prayer and Review of Prayer, though they are related. The Review of Prayer simply notes what happened in the prayer just finished. Repetition of Prayer, on the other hand, is itself a prayer experience that notes the movements felt in previous prayer and actually prays over them. It heightens and furthers our previous prayer experiences and reveals the patterns of how God has touched us; it is truly an experience of Ignatian discernment.

So, it is clear that Repetition of Prayer is not (i) repeating the prayer, going over it as one repeats a study assignment; (ii) going back over the same matter to "dig up something new"; or (iii) having to cover all the earlier prayer material.

Some examples:

• From my Review of an earlier prayer, I notice that I felt consoled while reflecting on Jesus at the Last Supper. In my next prayer, I do a "Repetition" by praying again over the Last Supper to see how God is gracing me.

• I notice in a previous Review of Prayer on Jesus's baptism that he had his back to me and I felt fear. I do a "Repetition" by returning to the place where Jesus was turned away to see what is going on in me that is causing me fear.

• I notice in a previous Review of Prayer on Jesus's hidden life that I was filled with anxiousness and sadness. In my next prayer, I do a "Repetition" by returning to the hidden life to see if there is something in me that is causing me anxiousness and sadness.[*]

Repetition prevents prayer from being superficial. It deepens our prayer experiences and sharpens our sensitivity to what God is communicating to us. It homes in on and fine tunes our experience of the inbreaking of the mystery of God in us.

How often might one do a Repetition? There is no set answer. We do repetitions when something seems to call us back to previous prayer experiences. It might be a feeling of consolation or desolation. It might be a kind of urging to look again at what was happening to us before, or it might be some feelings of uneasiness. There is no one way God guides us in prayer; the best we can do is be aware of what we are feeling and pray over it, pray into it. So only the pray-er will know when a Repetition might be fruitful.

Reflection:

    1) How has this exercise impacted the quality of your presence to others?

---

[*] See *Canadian Manual*, pp. R73-74.

2) Through Repetition of Prayer, desolation often breaks through to consolation.
3) Do a Repetition of Prayer on earlier prayer exercises to see what more God may wish to reveal to you.
4) Using the Scriptures above, pray for the grace to grow in deep confidence and trust in God's personal love and care for you.

Creative Activity: Pray some formal prayers that help deepen for you the grace of this exercise.

Grace Received: What did God reveal to you through this exercise? (See pages xii f. in the Foreword).

> *The spirituality of our community is centered*
> *on Christ and on participation in the Paschal Mystery.*
> *Our spirituality draws its life from*
> *the Sacred Scriptures,*
> *the liturgy,*
> *the doctrinal development of the Church,*
> *and the revelation of God's will in our times.*

—General Principles, #5.
(See below, p. 118).

Fourteen: Silence

Using the Scriptures given, pray for the grace to open your heart to yourself and to God.
- *Mk. 6:30-33 (Jesus and his disciples alone)*
- *Mt. 6:31 (do not be anxious)*
- *1 Jn. 3:20 (God is greater than our hearts)*
- *Ps. 46 (be still and know that I am God).*

A Jesuit who worked in northern Alaska told the story of his visit to two old Eskimo women. He greeted them with, "How are you?" Silence. He followed with, "Cold weather we're having." Silence. He added, "What's happening with your family?" One woman turned to the other and said, "Talk, talk, talk." Their culture, until the advent of television, was one of silence. One can only imagine the world of two and three hundred years ago in which the sounds the American Indians heard in this continent were mostly wind, water, and the human voice.

Silence in our society is viewed as abnormal, as something unnatural, something to be avoided, something odd, something to be ended. Campgrounds are invaded by radios. Television is watched endlessly, and hikers are wired to their Walkmans. Silence is unknown, feared, suspect.

And yet the pre-condition of all spiritual growth is silence. The experience of God requires time spent within our interior world. This is true even regarding the experience of nature. Spirituality is like breathing: the experience of God is not only found in going out (activity and involvement), but is also the fruit of coming in (reflection and prayer). Spirituality is the experience of reaching out and drawing in, of breathing out and breathing in.

The fact of tension and fatigue in our culture testifies to the absence of this balance, and seeing people fall profoundly silent while watching the sunset on the ocean confirms this truth. We need times of silence and solace for renewal; we are made for reflection, integration, and self-possession.

Silence can be experienced on different levels. The first of these levels is the absence of noise. People seek this kind of silence by fleeing noisy daily life and going into places of calm and solitude: mountains, the countryside, a den room, or a quiet chapel. This often produces a feeling of becoming relaxed, of an interior calm and recollection.

A second level of silence is in the experience of becoming aware of oneself, of feeling a great quiet and peace in the disappearance of anxiety and in the calming of the mind and imagination. This interior state is the relaxation that comes when, far from being possessed by things, one comes into possession of oneself. There is the experience of a sudden state of solitude with oneself and communion with many friends at one and the same time. In these privileged moments, one enjoys a great interior freedom and, at the same time, a striking communion with others.

A third level of silence is the coming to awareness, even in the midst of noise, of an all-embracing total presence. This perception, spontaneous and deep, quickly becomes a waiting, a desire, even a love, opening on a world that is mysterious, interior, and limitless. Sometimes it is a secret encounter which leaves behind an inexplicable joy and peace as one leaves a church. It may be an illumination of the mind in an instant, almost outside time, which brings a comprehension of many things, a comprehension one cannot unravel. Though momentary, it leaves behind prolonged traces in our ordinary life. This level of silence does not issue in grand thoughts or in precise projects or in the security of something definitely acquired. Such a presence comes to us as pure gift. It can be received only by simply welcoming it. That presence is God.

This exercise invites you to enter into the experience of silence. It takes patience, which is part of the experience of silence; and it can be done only gently and without hurry. It would be psychically schizophrenic to be able to move instantly from busyness and noise to silence. No; the movement is gradual, requiring an appropriate place and adequate time before becoming quiet. This movement grows out of practice, out of familiarity with the effort, and out of reaping the fruit that is found in silence.[*]

Reflection:
1) How has this exercise helped you in your service to others?
2) Try entering into silence.
   - Close your eyes, and relax your muscles from your feet to the top of your head. Take deep breaths and use whatever method works for you.
   - Remain relaxed, aware of your breathing. As you breathe out, say a word, such as "Spirit."
   - Do this for a sufficient period of time, and then gently ease yourself out of it back to where you were.
3) Do not use an alarm or worry about success. Let distractions flow by like boats down a river.
4) Using the scriptures, continually pray for the grace to be open to yourself, to one another, and to God.

Activity: Experience silence in the dark, perhaps during the night.

Grace Received: Do you feel you have been deepened in the grace you have been praying for throughout this exercise? What grace from the past two weeks are you particularly grateful for?

---

[*] See *Canadian Manual*, pp. 65-66.

*The local community
is the most appropriate
for a communal continuation of the dynamics
of the Spiritual Exercises.
These small communities practice
the type of prayer and relationships
which foster a process of integration of faith and life
by offering to all members
a permanent communal verification
of their spiritual and apostolic growth.*
—from General Norms, #39a.

Fifteen: Silence as Prayer

With the help of the scriptures that are given, pray for the grace of the experience of silence as opening our hearts to ourselves, to one another, and to God.

- *Ps. 139:13-18 (you formed my inmost being)*
- *Mt. 11:28-29 (come to me and rest)*
- *Mk. 1:12-13 (Jesus goes into the desert)*
- *Mk. 1:35 (Jesus goes off alone to pray)*
- *Mk. 6:30 (come and rest yourselves).*

There is a strong tendency to think that growth in our relationship with God is a consequence of accumulated spiritual experiences. It is true that such growth can follow spiritual effort, but it is not caused by it.

John of the Cross, in the sixteenth century, understood this well. For him, spiritual growth begins with the absence of not only material but also spiritual attachments. He saw that spiritual growth was a matter of peeling off, not adding on. In other words, we do not have to read such-and-so a book, or make some particular retreat, or have this particular spiritual director in order to deepen our relationship with God. We need, instead, to strip off this dependency, get rid of that attachment. The experience of God is already within us, waiting for us to come to it. And a great means for our doing this is silence.

Silence simply and inevitably leads us to our deepest self. It is where prayer happens, even if only for a moment. Silence of the mind and tongue makes us attentive to the One who is within. Silence is not "not speaking"; it is listening for God. In it we pass beyond ourselves and plunge into the mystery of God. Silence breathes God's presence.

Silence is not an experience of emptiness or embarrassment, but of fullness and richness. The temptation is to run from this. The fear is that at my deepest level, I will discover evil and not good, a deep dark pit. Until I resolve that question, a fundamental anxiety will remain within me.

It is no wonder, then, that silence can be threatening, or that it is counter-cultural in our society. It leads us past our distractions and defenses and brings us naked before ourselves, face to face with God. Silence leads us into the wellsprings of peace and being loved, which is the embrace of God.

Silence leads us to God wherever it happens and however we come into it. It can happen when we are sitting before a fire at the end of an enjoyable day, when we find ourselves simply being there, without thought or even self-awareness; it can happen when we go off by ourselves to ponder tragedy or some sorrowful event. In either case, or in others like them, God is present, and our becoming aware of this increases silence's fruit within us.

When we are in silence long enough, then, we find that we are not alone, that we are held in existence and loved. In silence, we are able to look past our struggles and fears and find the Holy One within. At that point our false self with its compulsiveness for importance and relevance disappears and our true self appears—people who are good and loveable, marked by a trust that we are loved, even in spite of what we do or think.

In silence, we discover what is true, see what is beautiful, and experience what is good. In silence we break free of our fear and make friends with our weakness; we shed what is shallow and embrace what is real. In silence we drop beneath what is intense and enter what is profound, we stand before the mystery of God and become aware of God's awareness of us. In silence we encounter God, we digest the experience of God, we are in relationship with God. In silence is prayer.[*]

---

[*] For more on this topic, see Henri Nouwen, *The Way of the Heart: A Desert Spirituality* (New York: Seabury Press, 1981).

Reflection:
1) How has prayerful silence helped you in your life's mission?
2) How comfortable are you with silence? What are its graces for you and what fears does it cause in you?
3) Repeat the previous exercise in silence and, rather than focusing on your relaxation, be aware of the presence of God within you.
4) Using the scriptures given above pray continually for the grace to experience silence as opening your heart to yourself, to one another, and to God.

Ritual: Use a candle and incense in a darkened environment to help you experience the grace of this exercise.

Grace Received: What is the grace given you during this exercise? How did the Spirit move you? This will be the focus of your faith-sharing in the next meeting.

Each of us receives from God a call
to make Christ and his saving action
present to our surroundings.
This personal apostolate is indispensable
for extending the Gospel
in a lasting and penetrating way
among the great diversity of persons, places, and situations.
—From General Principles, #8a.

Sixteen: Prayer as Relationship

Using the scripture passages given, pray for the grace to experience prayer as relationship to God.
- *Ps. 139:1-18 (you knit me in my mother's womb)*
- *Hos. 11:1-4, 8-11 (when Israel was a child)*
- *Lk. 13:34-35 (how I have yearned to gather you as a bird gathers her chicks)*
- *Jn. 15:1-6 (the vine and the branches)*
- *Jn. 15:15 (I call you friends).*

Prayer is being in relationship with God. It is like being with a person whom I love: a parent, a friend, a sibling, a wife, a husband.

This relational notion of prayer—being in relationship with God, or being drawn into relationship by God—is something easily missed by those who think that one must say prayers "in order" to have a relationship with God. Such people look upon prayer as a sort of prerequisite, an initiation rite to be performed before being able to approach God.

Such an attitude profoundly affects our prayer, for our image of God directly influences how we approach God. If God is someone who is to be appeased or who accepts only the worthy, then our prayer will be a kind of proving ground to win God's acceptance. We will then worry that our prayers, which will mostly be memorized, be said correctly and frequently enough. We will judge our prayer experiences as good or bad, and we will view our distractions as proof that God will not yet accept us. Again, this reduces prayer to a sort of pre-spiritual experience that tries to earn entry into God's friendship.

But that would not be prayer. That is fear and self-absorption. God is one who looks on us tenderly and with absolute love, seeing the funny things we do out of the best of intentions. God reads our desires and not our performances, accepting us just as we are, drawing us into relationship with the Divinity. This is the experience of prayer.

From the other side, being in a relationship with another reveals the experience of prayer. Now, being in relationship is experienced in many ways. It is experienced, for instance: (i) in a simple glance, a small gesture which revivifies the presence without apparent importance but whose sudden disappearance would leave us cold; (ii) in the longing to be with the one loved, in the waiting for that person's return or in reconciling after a quarrel; (iii) in the conversation after a tiring day after everyone else has gone to bed, sharing both sorrows, joys, disappointments, and hopes; (iv) in projects done with a friend; (v) in the moments of closeness and intimacy lived in silence or in the sharing of social life; (vi) in a walk with someone I trust and with whom I can share deeply. In any such relationship, there is a quality of caring, faithfulness, and commitment to each other.

These experiences of loving another are metaphors of how we love and are in relationship with God. Prayer is being in relationship with God—in sharing small experiences, in longing to be together, in projects done together, in moments of intimacy in silence and in activity—with God. This is prayer. Prayer does not happen outside of me—in obeying rules and focusing on my moral and ethical performance. My moral and ethical life will be holy when I am prayerful. Being moral and caring and loving are gifts of being in relationship with God. This relationship I foster through conscious effort, which is called prayer. It is not something I accomplish on my own. It is something I am invited into, that I receive, that I surrender into. It is gift.[*]

---

[*] See *Canadian Manual*, p. R69.

Reflection:
   1) How has your relationship with others affected your
      prayer as "relationship with God"?
   2) In Scripture God is described as the Spouse of Israel, as
      the mother of a child, as a lover. The Church is called
      the Spouse of God. The people of God are called
      Christ's body. Which of these images help you under-
      stand your prayer as being in relationship with God?
   3) How in practice do you find the time and conditions for
      nurturing your relationship with God?

Ritual: Use movement and gesture to express your relationship
with God as it is now, and then use them to express what you
would like this relationship to be. Do this alone and then with
a trusted friend.

Grace Received: What has God revealed to you during this
time? Is it the grace that you have been praying for?

> *The way of life of Christian Life Community*
> *commits its members,*
> *with the help of the community,*
> *to strive for a continuing personal and social growth*
> *which is spiritual, human, and apostolic.*
> *In practice, this involves*
> *participation in the Eucharist whenever possible;*
> *an active sacramental life;*
> *daily practice of personal prayer,*
> *especially that based on Sacred Scripture;*
> *discernment by means of daily review of one's life*
> *and, if possible, regular spiritual direction;*
> *an annual interior renewal*
> *in accordance with the sources of our spirituality;*
> *and a love for the mother of God.*
> —General Norms, #12a.

Seventeen: Stages of Growth in Prayer

With the help of the following scriptures, pray for the grace to deepen your relationship with God.
- *Mt. 16:21-28 (woman, you have great faith)*
- *Lk. 11:5-13 (seek and you shall find)*
- *Jn. 17:21 (I pray that all may be one).*

The exercises in this handbook are not a treatment of distinct and separate spiritual realities; rather, they are different views of the same truth. They are analogous to an experience the author once had while camping near Crater Lake, in southern Oregon. For three days he hiked around that lake, looking at it from every possible angle, even going down to its edge to touch the water. By the time the camping trip was over, the lake was a far more personal reality to him than it was at his first glimpse of it, shortly after his arrival.

Prayer, too, is a varied and richly textured experience: of asking, of receiving, of loving, of watching Jesus, of being (in other words) in relationship with God. Each experience of prayer is related to another; each is implied in every other. In fact, each fills out and completes the total experience of prayer, in the same fashion that the different viewpoints added to the experience of Crater Lake.

The present exercise compares growth in prayer to growth in a human friendship—a good comparison, since prayer is the experience of friendship with God. This growth in prayer is a matter of degree, not of kind. The very first stages of prayer are no less a true experience of God than are its later, more developed stages. Growth in prayer has to do with the maturing of our relationship with God, something which comes to us not as a result of our own efforts but rather as gift. We receive prayer; we are led into a deeper and more matured relationship with God.

Let us, then, look at the similarities between growth in a human friendship and growth in prayer. One can note stages in each.

Stages in Growth in Relationship with Another:

- The *first* is the desire and openness to meet the other.
- The *second* involves a meeting of minds: coming to know more "about" each other. Silence is awkward, and there is the beginning of shared experience.
- The *third* involves a meeting of the hearts, knowing that this new relationship should develop. Silence becomes eloquent, and there is a softness in the voice.
- The *fourth* involves shared feelings, verbal and non-verbal; small gestures say a lot. There is more shared silence and a greater affective energy invested in each other.
- The *fifth* involves a quieted sensible and emotional level. There is a re-investment at a deeper level, reflecting an older relationship.

Stages in Growth in One's Relationship to God:

- The *first stage* is the readiness to open up to God. There is a feeling of not being satisfied, of an emptiness within.
- The *second stage* is characterized by vocal prayer, using set formulae. The meaning here is in the words, and the person is done when hitting the "amen." Silence is awkward in prayer.
- The *third stage* is marked by a boredom with vocal and memorized prayer. The pray-er becomes tired of saying them. This is the first critical moment. There is an invitation to deepen. It would be a mistake to give up on prayer.
- The *fourth stage* is discursive, going from thought to thought, using a prayer or scripture passage, following both mental and affective progress. There are

feelings here, and silence becomes more important.

- The *fifth stage* is less discursive, less moving from point to point. There is less of a need for material for prayer, and what is used provides a deeper experience. Vocal prayer is more difficult, and there is desire for more silence.

- The *sixth stage* is marked by less sensible feelings. Doubts arise; there is a feeling of wasting time, and one is tempted to less effort. This is the second critical moment. A purification of feelings is going on, moving from the consolations of God to God's own self. This is a movement to deeper faith. Remain faithful in prayer, to its time and length. Use vocal prayer to help focus. Also, read spiritual books, though not getting into simply reading. Do not escape the silence; the dryness is a gift. God is being re-chosen on a deeper level.

- The *seventh stage* involves a sense of the presence of God more and more, like air and water. There is a state of recollection with frequent contacts with God. There is deep peace, even in dryness. Vocal prayer is now the experience of being together, of gratitude, not one of "having to recharge." There is now great value in vocal prayer, gesture, and movement as enfleshing the interior.

Throughout these stages of growth in prayer is a corresponding development in motives for prayer: from being told to pray, to sensible experiences leading to prayer, to doing so out of belief in one's faith, to shared experience in gratitude.

It is critical to remember not to judge prayer. The above is descriptive, simply highlighting the similarity between one's relationship with God and one's relationship with a friend. The focus of prayer is on God, not on ourselves. It is not achieved through analysis; it is a gift into which we are invited, into which we surrender.[*]

Reflection
1) Does the quality of your presence to others call you to a deeper relationship with God?
2) What is the quality of your relationship with God?
3) What would you like this relationship to be?

Symbol: Find an object, something that is yours or from nature, that expresses the movements of the grace you have received.

Graces Received: How were you moved affectively during your prayer these past two weeks? What grace are you being called to follow?

---

[*] From a series of lectures given by George A. Aschenbrenner, S.J., in the fall of 1983 at Gonzaga University, Spokane, Washington.

Eighteen: Community Reflection on Its Growth in Prayer

Using the scriptures provided, pray for the grace of a deep wonder and awe at our existence.
- *Dt. 7:7-9 (the Lord set his heart on you)*
- *Is. 54:5-10 (my love shall never leave you)*
- *Hos. 11:1-4,8-11 (when Israel was a child)*
- *Lk. 22:14-20 (institution of the Eucharist)*
- *Jn. 13:17 (washing of the feet)*

Exercises Seven through Seventeen have had to do with prayer: the Consciousness Examen, Praying for a Grace, Praying with Scripture, Review of Prayer, Ignatian Contemplation, Images of God, Repetition of Prayer, Silence, Silence as Prayer, Prayer as Relationship, and Stages of Growth in Prayer. Before moving into the next unit on following Jesus, it would be good for the community to reflect, both as individuals and as a community, on its life and growth during these past eleven exercises.

The following questions may be helpful for this:
- ◆ How have I experienced God's presence as a result of my participation in this community?
- ◆ What exercises from this unit on prayer struck me particularly?
- ◆ How has this experience affected me
  - in my relationship to others?
  - in my life of prayer?
  - in my desire to grow as a Christian?
  - in my commitment to Christ, to those around me, to this community?
- ◆ What growth have I seen within this group? In its striving to become Jesus's disciples?
- ◆ What issues do I feel need to be addressed by this community?
- ◆ Anything else?

Reflection:
1) You might consider doing a ritual for this meeting to celebrate the community's life together, ending with a party/social of some kind.
2) Using the scriptures given above, pray for the grace of deep wonder and awe at your existence.

Ritual: Place this book and the Bible on a table with a lit candle and sit quietly before them. How well do the two complement each other for you? (See below, p. 112f.)

Grace Received: What has God revealed to you about your own spiritual growth and that of your CLC community? Does this grace suggest future directions for you? (See the Foreword, p. xii f.)

Because our community is a way of Christian life,
these principles are to be interpreted
not so much by the letter of this text
as by the spirit of the Gospel and the interior law of love.
This law of love,
which the Spirit inscribes in our hearts,
expresses itself anew in each situation of our daily lives.
This Spirit-inspired love
respects the uniqueness of each personal vocation
and enables us to be open and free,
always at the disposal of God;

*it challenges us to see our responsibilities
and constantly to seek answers to the needs of our times,
to work together
with the entire People of God and all people of good will
to seek progress and peace,
justice and charity,
liberty and dignity for all.*

—General Principles, #2.

(See below, page 117.)

Part Three

Following Jesus

Nineteen: Mary, Mother and Disciple

With the help of the scriptures that are given, pray for the grace to become a companion of Mary.
- *Lk. 1-2 (the infancy narrative)*
- *Jn. 2:1-12 (the wedding feast at Cana)*
- *Lk. 2:51-52 (the hidden life)*
- *Jn. 19:25-27 (Mary at the foot of the cross).*

Mary holds a special place of reverence for Saint Ignatius, as she does also for the Society of Jesus and Christian Life Communities whose spiritual quests are inspired by the spirit and vision of Ignatius.

Throughout the centuries of Christianity, however, Mary has had a checkered history, being viewed in various ways and being held in varying degrees of regard. She has been seen at one time as the heart of the Christian community, at another its mediator. She has been seen as other-worldly and unreal, and then again as human. She has been looked upon as weak and again as strong. To be sure, the images people have of Mary, no less than those they have of God, may well have arisen out of particular circumstances and backgrounds. But, however Mary has been viewed, she has remained next to her Son as central to the Christian tradition.

At a time when scholarly research and Christian education have become commonly available to the believing Christian, it becomes more imperative to move away from sentimental and semi-magical representations of Mary to ones that are authentic and real. Focusing exclusively on the person of Mary must give way to focusing also on her mission. For it is her mission that gives prominence to her as a woman; it is her relationship to Jesus that illuminates her meaning as a person. And so we can ask:

Who is Mary? We know nothing of her physical features. We do know that she lived in a small village without distinction, a woman tied to her home and devoted to her family. We also know that she was independent and courageous, traveling some 72 miles to visit Elizabeth. She was devoted to the biblical formation of her son, to the point that he already stood out in his learning at the age of twelve.

She married the carpenter of the village and had one son, a fact which possibly left her somewhat inferior in the eyes of the other women who measured their blessings by the number of children they bore their husbands. She watched her son discredited, accused of being a criminal, and executed. From the outside, the life of Mary was a complete failure.

Who is Mary? But there is another side to Mary's life—her faith. The annunciation was the central event in her life, the foundational experience of her faith; and she did not find it easy. Immediately after it took place, in fact, she knew that what was laid out to her would be difficult, would be a sacrifice.

For she had dreamed of her marriage to Joseph and, as a faithful Israelite, had entertained visions of bearing him many sons. And now she would lose her husband; she would lose her honor in front of the whole village and be exposed to the full rigor of the law, which was death by stoning for unfaithful brides.

And yet she said, "Let it be done to me as you say." She accepted her vocation and fully opened herself to her mission. She shows us the tremendous vital force that flows from seeking one's true vocation and offering it in mission. Fanatical devotional views of Mary have made her unreal, untouchable, safe. In reality she is a paradigm of faith, an archetype of mission, a model of church. She does not show forth simply a doctrine of faith; she shows forth a life of faith. At issue with Mary is spirituality.

Mary teaches us that through faith, promise becomes reality. Her mission she received from God; she did not take it up on her own. And she achieved that mission silently, tenaciously, serenely, fully inserted into the life of her people and into the social and political context of her country. She carried out her mission in the routines of everyday life common to the women around her. Her faith took root in daily existence. She neither took refuge in tranquil contemplation nor lost contact with her faith through external activity. She echoed her divine inspiration in the hard efforts of her new mission. She was a contemplative in action.[*]

Reflection:
1) How have your life of faith and your experience of Mary affected each other?
2) What has been your image of Mary? Who is she to you now? What are you attracted to most in her?

---

[*] See *Canadian Manual,* pp. R82-84.

One might note, in passing, that one aspect of Mary with which most Christians and many non-Christians are familiar is that of her reported apparitions to certain individuals. Down through the centuries, there have been numerous reports of apparitions by Mary, each claiming to provide a message for the people of that time. Some contain pleadings for prayer and conversion, and others threats of punishment. Many spectacular events have accompanied these events, including personal conversions, healings, and physical phenomena of one kind or other. Church authorities study these claims carefully, and are anything but hasty in declaring them authentic.

Some find themselves concerned about the urgency that these warnings contain. Without going into the question of the authenticity of these claims, one needs merely to recall that the urgency for the need for conversion is already quite clearly contained in the Gospel. The full revelation of God is already there, and the centrality of Jesus already established. Any subsequent authentic spiritual event merely confirms it.

Act: Do a mantra: a word or short phrase that is repeated frequently as a prayer—such as "Mary," or "Jesus, son of Mary, have mercy on me," and the like.

Grace Received: What grace did you receive during your prayer over this exercise? Is this a new grace for you?

> *Mary's co-operation with God*
> *begins with her "yes" in the mystery of the*
> *Annunciation-Incarnation.*
> *Her effective service,*
> *as shown in her visit to Elizabeth,*
> *and her solitude with the poor,*
> *as reflected in the Magnificat*
> *make her our inspiration to act for justice in the world today.*
> —General Principles, #9
> (See below, p. 119f.)

Twenty: Peter the Disciple

*With the help of the scriptures that are given, pray for the grace
to become a disciple of Jesus like Peter.*
- *Lk. 5:1-11 (the call of Peter)*
- *Mt. 14:22-23 (Jesus walks on water)*
- *Mt. 16:13-20 (Peter the rock)*
- *Mt. 17:1-13 (the transfiguration)*
- *Mt. 18:21-22 (Peter asks about forgiveness).*

What can we say about Peter? He is as real and tangible as
any figure in the Gospels. He embodies qualities and charac-
teristics with which almost everyone can identify: he was real,
ordinary, impetuous, and vulnerable; he was headstrong,
generous, determined, and loving. He was strong and he was
weak; he saw and he was blind; he was unpredictable and he
was faithful. He thought he could walk on water, and he
needed Jesus to save him from drowning. He attacked the
servant with his sword in the Garden of Olives, and he
cowered before a servant girl in Herod's courtyard. He
identified Jesus as the Messiah, the Son of the Living God; and
he denied three times that he even knew Him.

Peter promised to remain faithful to Jesus even in Jerusa-
lem, and he wept at betraying Him. He saw Jesus transfigured,
and he saw Him crucified. He recognized Jesus by the
seashore after the resurrection; he professed three times that
he loved Him, and he was chosen by Jesus to be the leader of
the little Nazarean community and the first-generation Church.

But, again as with Mary, it is not in his personhood that
Peter's primary spiritual significance is to be found, but rather
in how he lived out his faith in his friend Jesus, and how in
turn Jesus guided him.

The grace we should pray for in this exercise is "to become
a disciple of Jesus like Peter." But which Peter? The one who
was proud and unfaithful, or the one who was humbled and

filled with repentant love for Jesus? It is true that we do not ordinarily model ourselves on people at their weakest; but there is also something about seeing another's weakness that reveals our own, as well as God's love for us. Peter's weaknesses and failures were not his enemies. They were the medium for his own self-discovery, and his admitting his shortcomings led him to Jesus. The depth of his knowing Jesus came not so much from his witnessing of Jesus's transfiguration as it did from his triple denial of Jesus in which he experienced his absolute need for Jesus to save him.

Let us hope that we can be like Peter, who through his weaknesses came to know Jesus. For all too often, we who smile at Peter's foibles frown at our own: ours are too real and painful for us to ignore. We too know what it means to be impetuous and vulnerable, blind and unpredictable, brave and afraid. In fact, we can become so preoccupied with how bad we are that we miss how good we are.

But, as in the case of Peter, our weaknesses and failures are not our enemies. It is through recognizing our false selves that we come to know our true selves. "Let the weeds grow until the harvest, lest in pulling them out you pull out the good wheat as well." Then, like Peter, we too will come to experience Jesus loving us, not because we do all things well but because He loves us—loves us unconditionally.

Some questions may be helpful for the exercise.

♦ Who is Peter to you? Can you identify with him? How?
♦ What in Peter makes you uncomfortable about yourself?
♦ What about Peter makes you hopeful and uplifted in faith?
♦ What does following Jesus involve?

Reflection
1) How have your doubts and weaknesses affected your being a disciple of Jesus like Peter?
2) Ask Peter to be a companion with you. Spend time with

him in his life, and ask him to spend time with you in yours. Watch and listen to him.

3) Using the scriptures given above, pray to become a follower of Christ like Peter.

Symbol: Be in the presence of water—the ocean, a lake, a stream, a bowl. Trace your hand through it. Picture Peter walking on water at Jesus's bidding. Ask Peter to help you see the depth of your faith in Jesus. Ask yourself what you are doing for Jesus, and what you would like to do for Him.

Grace Received: What struck you from this exercise? What grace of following Jesus have you received? What grace do you desire? This will be the focus of your faith-sharing at your next meeting.

Our community is made up of Christians:
men and women, adults and youth,
of all social conditions
who want to follow Jesus Christ more closely
and work with him for the building of the Kingdom,
who have recognized Christian Life Community
as their particular vocation with the Church.
We propose to commit ourselves as Christians
in bearing witness to those human and Gospel values
within the Church and society
which affect the dignity of the person,
the welfare of the family,
the integrity of creation.
We are especially aware of the pressing need
to work for justice

through a preferential option for the poor
and a simple life style
which expresses our freedom and solidarity with them.
To prepare ourselves more effectively
for apostolic witness and service in our daily environment,
we assemble in community those
who feel a more urgent need to unite their human life
in all its dimensions
with the fullness of their Christian faith.
Responding to the call of Christ and following our charism,
we seek to achieve this unity of life
in the world in which we live.

—General Principles, #4
(See below, page 118.)

Twenty-One: Following Jesus

With the help of the scriptures that are given, pray for the grace to become a disciple of the Jesus who is still crucified and rises today.

- *Lk. 9:23-26 (condition of discipleship)*
- *Lk. 10:1-20 (mission of the seventy-two)*
- *Jn. 13:12-17 (no disciple is greater than the master)*
- *Jn. 15:9-77 (a disciple's love).*

Following Jesus:

When we looked Mary and Peter, we saw that following Jesus is more than simply following a leader. Jesus's invitation to us to become his followers involves for us, as it did for Mary and Peter, not only being with Jesus but being like Him. We do this by internalizing his values, thoughts, and ways throughout our entire being, and by making his operational attitudes our own: "I live no longer, but Jesus lives in me."

Jesus lived for others. And so it would be an error to confine our following of Him simply to our own daily concerns. Focusing only on our personal and spiritual growth erects a barrier between our lives and the life that pulses in humanity. As members of Christ's body, we are so linked and interrelated with one another that our tasks, dedication, and commitments are no longer ours; they belong to the whole church. This involves a passage from a life in which moral obligations are the dominant concern to a spiritual life in which the acts of God are made visible through us. "The Son can do nothing alone; the Son only sees and does what the Father is doing; and whatever the Father does the Son does too" (Jn. 5:19).

But following Jesus involves a paradox. On the one hand, being Jesus's followers fills us with energy and love. It is not a depressing experience; it is one filled with meaning and peace. It is the way of invitation and freedom—so much so that were we to feel forced to follow Jesus, or were we to follow Him out of a fear and a guilt which turn us in on ourselves, we can be sure that this would not be the action of grace or the experience of being his followers. On the other hand, being Jesus's disciple can also be difficult and even threatening. The freedom found in following Him does not necessarily replace fear. How, then, can I be peaceful when I am afraid? Mary, Peter, and others down to our own day show us that it is possible, that the attraction to Jesus is stronger than any resistance or fear that we may feel. In fact, remaining faithful to Him especially when we are afraid actually manifests great freedom and love.

There is nothing unusual about this. How often parents embrace pain and stress to bring a son to life or to nurture a daughter to adulthood. So it is with being a follower of Jesus. The attraction to serving Him will be deeper and more powerful than any obstacle or danger perceived, and it is the journey of our faith that brings that power and love in us to action.

Being a companion of Jesus, moreover, is a grace we receive. It is not something achieved through our own efforts. Being his follower is a gift; and the more we receive this grace, the freer we will be to follow Him. We will know how Jesus is inviting us through what attracts us, by the fire that we feel for life. Following Jesus gives our lives meaning; it is offered out of love and its gift is freedom.

CLC, in turn, is all about helping its members overcome fear of and resistance to being followers of Jesus, in serving in word and action where they live. The practice of the Consciousness Examen helps its members, both individually and as a community, to discover the apostolic meaning that is to be found in the most humble realities of daily life. Our life finds its permanent inspiration in the Gospel of the poor and humble Christ. Living in accord with this, we will no longer be tempted (or even able) to separate what is Christian from what is "secular" any more than we could separate what is God from what is human in the person of Christ.

Following Jesus and Community:

The values of Society are not the values of Jesus. People say, "Everybody is doing it . . . . The message of Jesus is too idealistic." The criticism and ridicule, and the doubts that they raise, are translated into many little dyings that the follower of Jesus will face. The support of other people is crucial for the disciple to remain faithful to living out the Gospel. The acceptance, affirmation, and trust found in a community inspire in us the courage to do this.

It is significant that Jesus's disciples spent time with one another. Rarely did He send them out alone; He sent them two by two. Following Jesus calls us into relationship. "How can we say we love God whom we cannot see if we do not love those whom we do see?" (1 Jn. 4:20). Jesus's followers were a small group who loved and affirmed one another. The modern disciple cannot hope to go it alone. The two examples from the Gospel of people who tried to do so were Judas and Peter, just before the death of Jesus. Following Jesus builds a community of people who share the values, thoughts, and lifestyle of Jesus.[*]

Reflection:

1) Has your concern for others increased your desire to be a disciple of Jesus, like Mary and Peter?
2) What does following Jesus mean in your life? What gives you joy, and what causes you struggle?
3) What kind of following of Jesus would you like to characterize your life, and who supports you in it?

---

[*] See *Canadian Manual*, pp. R85-89.

4) Using the scriptures given above, pray to become a follower of the Jesus who is still crucified and rises today.

Activity: Listen to music that inspires you, that inspires you to be a true follower of Jesus. (See below, p. 115.)

Grace Received: Is the grace you prayed for the grace you received? Where does the grace you received lead you in prayer?

Twenty-Two: Preferential Option for the Poor

With the help of the scriptures given, pray for the grace to recognize and serve Christ in the poor.
- *Amos 1:2, 2:7 (Yahweh raises up the lowly)*
- *Micah 6:8 (act, love, and walk with God)*
- *Mt. 25:31-46 (what you do to the least, you do to me)*
- *Lk. 10:25-37 (the good Samaritan)*
- *Jn. 13:1-15 (washing of the feet).*

The truth that we are constantly striving to see is that God is in all things, the same God in others as in me, the same God in good times as in hard, the same God in the wealthy as in the poor. Native religions speak of "the Spirit that moves in all things," which highlights the sacredness of all creation. God is not constrained within a certain economic structure or political system or country. God is in all things: the good and the bad, the just and the unjust, my friends and my enemies. "The sun rises on the bad and the good. God rains on the just and the unjust" (Mt. 5:45).

The Hebrew covenant testifies to the special care and love to be shown to the poor and the weak:

Concerning Israel, the pastures of the shepherds will languish, and the summit of Carmel wither . . . because they trample the heads of the weak into the dust of the earth, and force the lowly out of the way (Amos 1:2, 2:7). Yahweh raises up the lowly from the dust; from the dunghill the poor, to seat them with princes (Ps. 113:7-8). The spirit of Yahweh is upon me . . . to bring glad tidings to the lowly . . . to proclaim liberty to captives and release to the prisoners (Is. 61:1).

The Christian covenant reflects the same love and concern:

God has anointed me to preach the gospel to the

poor (Lk. 4:18). Blessed are the poor, the lowly,
the hungry, for the reign of God is theirs (Mt. 5:3-
12). Whatever you do to the least of these, you do
to me (Mt. 25:31-46).

The poor reveal the Gospel to us; we cannot experience
conversion without turning to the poor. Poverty is the choice
of Christ, the choice of God, the way of God among us. We
reach out to the poor because we need to; the reign of God is
revealed in the lowly. In our ministry to them, the poor
minister to us by revealing our poverty, our fears, and our
attachments. The poor reveal our need for God; they are a gift
to us. Our need for God reveals the poor, and our ministering
to them becomes a gift to us. It is a circle. This is why the
preferential option for the poor is much more than an obligation to be fulfilled—it is a grace to be prayed for.[*]

None the less, the notion of a preferential option for the
poor can be an upsetting, disturbing one. There can be and is
much fear of it, and resistance to looking at it. It frequently
raises feelings of guilt for possessing more than others, as if
poverty in itself had an intrinsic value. It easily produces
feelings of fear of having to work with the homeless and the
addicted on our inner-city streets, as if everyone should be
able to do everything.

When such fears and suspicions turn us in on ourselves and
paralyze us into inaction, they must be seen for the deceptions
they are. True, feeling unsettled about the growing gap
between the rich and the poor is healthy; and caring about the
welfare of the destitute is hopeful. But working on behalf of
the poor out of guilt and a feeling of coercion helps no one,
including ourselves. We know that the Spirit invites us not by
guilt or force but by attraction. Reaching out to others must

---

[*] For the complete text from which this is taken, see "The Disturbing
Subject: the Option for the Poor," *Studies in the Spirituality of Jesuits* (St.
Louis: Seminar on Jesuit Spirituality), XXI n.2 (March, 1989).

follow our dispositions and abilities; it is an extension of who we most deeply and truly are. It is therefore deeply personal and individual. It is a gift, a grace, a revelation of the meaning and joy of Jesus's mission.

But it is a demanding gift, an insistent grace. Fr. Peter-Hans Kolvenbach, the Superior General of the Jesuits, observed that, "The new commandment means the gift of one's being, of one's person. As long as we give only of our possessions, we have given nothing. It is necessary to give one's life in the model of Christ."

What the preferential option for the poor adds to all this is an attitude, a way of seeing and acting. It means that I have an automatic bias in favor of the poor in what I do and see done. It means that I live a lifestyle that helps lessen the gap between the rich and the poor. It states that all political and business decisions should be made only after first asking the question, "How will what we do here affect the poor?" Then we look around and pray for the grace to know how we are to show our preferential option for the poor.[*]

---

[*] In the previous footnote, mention was made of the March, 1989, issue of *Studies in the Spirituality of Jesuits* (St. Louis: Seminar on Jesuit Spirituality, XXI, no.2) entitled *The Disturbing Subject: the Option for the Poor*). To be somewhat more specific, this number contains two essays that are of particular interest to us here (in addition to several other, briefer articles). One of these two is Adrien Demoustier, S.J., "The First Companions and the Poor" (pp. 4-20); the other, Jean-Yves Calvez, S.J., "The Preferential Option for the Poor: Where Does It Come From for Us?" (pp. 21-35). Given below is a summary of these two articles.

Who Were the Poor for St. Ignatius and the Early Society of Jesus?

The poor, in Ignatius's time, were the common people, the little people, those who worked in good times but without any margin of security, and also the destitute and beggars.

The poor, from the perspective of his religious vocation, were those who were not protected or who did not protect themselves from humiliation, and who achieved the humility which permitted genuinely free choices. "Blessed are the poor" was a rejection of society's standard as a criterion of decision.

Religious poverty, to Ignatius and his early companions, meant owning nothing as well as abdicating ownership of everything they used. Poverty became a sharing of goods and a public, institutional proclamation of evangelical fraternity and sharing. To carry on their work, they received from society the financial means to enter into its culture in order to evangelize it (DeMoustier, pp. 5-9).

The Beginning Society of Jesus and the Poor

Presence to the poor and action on their behalf were integral to the founding activity of the Society, quite as much as learned preaching, pastoral action, and spiritual direction. The condition of their mission to all people was the conversion of the powerful to a sense of social responsibility to those who needed temporal as well as spiritual relief. The great could not experience genuine conversion without turning to the poor.

The early companions' choice of proximity to the poor in living and work gave orientation to their presence to the great. During the winter famine of 1539-40, they gave the food they could gather to the poor and turned the large house in which they were living into accommodations for the homeless. Their ministry to the low was the intentional point of departure to their ministry to the high. Their mission to important people and institutions were almost like distractions from their normal work with the poor. They characteristically began with the poor and turned to the rich, striving for their conversion as the best means of reintegrating the marginalized into society. Their aim was to lead all to a sharing which evidenced a Gospel communion. It was starting from the destitute that it was possible to go to the rich (DeMoustier, pp. 11-17).

The Poor Today

The 32nd General Congregation of the Society of Jesus (1974-75) recommended solidarity of all Jesuits with the poor, with families who are of modest means who make up the majority of every country and who are often poor and oppressed. Its linking the promotion of justice with the service of faith is that from which the obligation of solidarity with the poor comes. The 33rd General Congregation (1983) spoke explicitly of the need for the preferential option for the poor as a characteristic of the whole mission of the Society.

Pope John Paul II, in his address to a group of cardinals in Rome on December 21, 1984, stated, "Engagement with the poor constitutes a dominant motif of my pastoral activity. I have made and do make this option. I identify with it. I feel it could not be otherwise, since it is the eternal message of the Gospel. That is the option Christ made." In his address to the Peruvian bishops on October 4 of that year, he emphasized his agreement with this precept: "The Church intends to maintain its preferential option for the poor and encourages the engagement of those who devote themselves selflessly to those most in need. That is an integral part of their mission." A few weeks earlier he had affirmed a similar position to the bishops of Paraguay: "It is true that the precept to love all men and women admits of no exclusion, but it does admit a privileged engagement in favor of the poorest" (Calvez, pp. 21-24).

Who Are the Poor in This Option?

Clearly this is a sensitive area. Some maintain it refers to those who lack a supportive community, as in drug addiction, prostitution, divorce, and unemployment. Others say it means primarily the economically poor. The Church in recent declarations adopts a rather wide interpretation of poverty. Poverty is almost synonymous with deprivation, such as material deprivation, unjust oppression, psychic and physical sickness such as cancer and AIDS, even death ("Christian Freedom and Liberation," Instruction of the Sacred Congregation for the Doctrine of the Faith; cf. *Origins*, 15 [1986], 713). The Church holds to the position, however, that a prominent place should be reserved for the poor, especially the economically poor, and for the victims of injustice for whom redress is possible. Even though there are many meanings, we cannot empty the word "poor" of its primary meaning (Calvez, pp. 24-26).

What Is Expected of Us?

Clearly, an attitude of love and compassion. This must be an active love, an effective one; "to relieve, to defend, to free" are the three verbs by which the instruction "Christian Freedom and Liberation" indicates what is expected of us with respect to the poor. This would require nothing less than defending and freeing victims of injustice.

Is this a call to share poverty? To relieve and fight against it? Or is it only a matter of developing an awareness of the situation of the poor? The latter would be something a bit too facile and would not square with the need to "relieve, defend, and free." The example of Jesus shows that he not only had compassion on the crowd who had nothing to eat; he fed them. A crucial phase in the document quoted above states, "This poverty is an evil from which humanity must be freed as completely as possible."

Some prefer "love of preference for the poor" to "preferential option." The document above does use this phrase, but it also speaks of effective remedial action, even to structural changes. The phrase "love of preference" does highlight the gratuity of the love. The head of the Jesuit order, Fr. Peter-Hans Kolvenbach, has however cautioned against making the preferential option for the poor "an egoistic enterprise, the manipulation of the misery of others to one's own profit or glory"—basically the poor for our satisfaction. "The new commandment means the gift of one's being, of one's person. As long as we give only of our possessions, we have given nothing. It is necessary to give one's life in the model of Christ" (Kolvenbach, speech "To the Worker Mission," Turin, August of 1985) (Calvez, pp. 24-28).

The Option for the Poor: the Service of Faith and the Promotion of Justice:

"Blessed are they who struggle for justice." There can be no human society if there is no concern for the most vulnerable. Christ revealed his "Father" in poverty, showing us in what consists true wealth. Poverty itself says something about God. Christ came close not only to those who had detachment of heart to await his coming, but to the poor of this world as well as those in deprivation from community, even if rich in worldly goods. In this is something which calls the Christian to special fraternity with the poor along with Christ in his own relationship with the poor. Fr. Pedro Arrupe, S.J., said at the World Eucharistic Congress in Philadelphia (1976) that "if there is hunger anywhere in the world, our celebration of the Eucharist is in some way incomplete everywhere" (Calvez, pp. 28-32).

Conclusion: These reflections on the preferential option for the poor are not likely to provide instant peace of mind. Their first effect is to make us feel ill at ease. With grace we can transcend the attitude which will not take a step because the road ends only in the infinite distance.

Reflection:
 1) How is your option for the poor reflected in you and in your relationships with others?
 2) Pray for the grace to be able to recognize and serve Christ in the poor.

Symbolic Ritual: Place different kinds of flowers on a table. Contemplate them until you see the beauty in all.

Grace Received: What grace have you received from your prayer in view of living with a preferential option for the poor? Do you fear this grace? Do you welcome it?

Everything changes when we understand the deepest nature of this call—that poverty is the choice of Christ, the choice of God, the way of God among us. The question is how can we recognize better Christ in the poor and thus serve them in order to serve Christ in them (Calvez, pp. 33-35).

Twenty-Three: Community Reflection on Its Growth in Following Jesus

With the help of the following scriptures, pray for the grace to grow in lovingly following Jesus.
- *Mt. 5:5 (blessed are the poor)*
- *Mt. 20:20-28 (the mother of James and John)*
- *Lk. 4:16-21 (the beginning of Jesus's ministry)*
- *Mt. 17:1-8 (the transfiguration).*

Exercises 24 through 27 had to do with the following of Jesus, considering: Mary, Mother and Disciple; Peter the Disciple; Following Jesus; and the Preferential Option for the Poor. Before moving on to the next unit (on the experience of God's unconditional love), it would be good for the community to reflect, both as individuals and as community, on its life and growth during the past four exercises.

The following questions may be helpful for this:

- ♦ How have I experienced God as a result of my being in this community?
- ♦ What exercises from this unit on following Jesus struck me particularly?
- ♦ How has this experience affected me:
  - in my presence to others?
  - in my community life and life of prayer?
  - in my desire to know and follow Christ more?
  - in my commitment to Christ, to those around me, to this community?
- ♦ What growth have I seen in this group? in its striving to be followers of Jesus?
- ♦ Is the community called to exercise common ministry?
- ♦ What issues do I feel need to be addressed by this community?
- ♦ Anything else?

Activity: Set up a prayer environment, such as candles, music, incense, crucifix, and so on, to use during your contemplative prayer.

Grace Received: What graces have you received during these past four exercises? Do you pray unceasingly that they may be deepened in you?

> *Because our Community is a way of Christian life,*
> *these principles are to be interpreted*
> *not so much by the letter of this text*
> *as by the spirit of the Gospel and the interior law of love.*
> *This law of love,*
> *which the Spirit inscribes in our hearts,*
> *expresses itself anew in each situation of our daily lives.*
> *This Spirit-inspired love respects the uniqueness*
> *of each personal vocation*
> *and enables us to be open and free,*
> *always at the disposal of God.*
> *It challenges us to see our responsibilities*
> *and constantly to seek answers to the needs of our times,*
> *to work together with the entire People of God*
> *and all people of good will*
> *to seek*
> *progress and peace,*
> *justice and charity,*
> *liberty and dignity*
> *for all.*

—General Principles, #2
(See below, page 117.)

Part Four

The Unconditional
Love of God

Twenty-Four: God's Unconditional Love

With the help of the scriptures given below, pray for the grace to embrace God's unconditional love.
- *Ps. 104 (praise the Creator)*
- *Ps. 96 (rejoice at God's gifts)*
- *Is. 49:15-16 (continual love of God)*
- *Jn. 3:1-16 (God so loved us)*
- *Jn. 13:31-35 (the new commandment).*

Spiritual growth lies in our becoming more and more available to God's love. God offers this continual, unconditional love to us, and we need only "be there" to receive it. Embracing this love is not something that we achieve by our own efforts; it is something that is given us, something that we are invited into, something that we surrender into.

God has always and forever loved us, with no strings attached. This is easy to say. It is difficult to accept. In fact, it is one of the most difficult truths to accept that we encounter. "Me? God loves me? How can God love me—I'm not even sure that I love myself!" We feel inadequate and unworthy; we feel that, somehow, we ought to be different from what we are if we are to be lovable. And so we are likely to lessen the impact of this truth by trivializing the word "loves" into something like "puts up with," thereby substituting for God's personal love for us something that is distant and impersonal. Indeed, in our society when we experience love, it is often a love that comes with many conditions attached to it: we are lovable if we dress in a certain way, if our hair is the right color, if we own a particular car, if we have a prestigious job.

But none of this is true with God. No matter how we look or act or what we think of ourselves, God loves us totally just as we are. We cannot lose that love, we cannot escape it, we cannot hide from it. All of creation is in fact an outpouring of God's love. We pray to see ourselves and all creation as a continual gift bringing us into a closer relationship with God. All is gift from God to lead us to God.

We don't experience this kind of love very often, and so when we do meet up with it, it can be frightening. Maybe, indeed, we won't let ourselves believe that God's love is what it is, since we fear its consequences. If we allow God to love us, then we need to love ourselves. Worse yet, we also need to love others, including those in our lives whom the Gospel refers to as our enemies, but whom we might refer to simply as "jerks." Why? Look at the example of Jesus. He not only had compassion on the hungry crowd, he fed them. He not only preached repentance, he healed people's hurts. He not only preached forgiveness, he forgave those who killed him—killed him because he loved them too much.

Or, we might find ourselves saying "If I love God totally, what will I have to give up? If I get too close, what will God ask of me? I'd better be careful what I pray for!—because if I allow God to love me, then what's going to happen to me?" We're afraid that we're going to be lost, swallowed up, drowned in love.

And yet we pray for God's love and want to experience it. God "adores" us, God wants us to melt away with this love.

This is both frightening and wonderful. We can accept God's loving a child unconditionally, but not God's loving ourselves. We need to spend time with those parts of ourselves which doubt this. It will be there that God's love is revealed; it will be then that even our doubting selves will be redeemed by God's grace and we will become open to God's love for us.

For how can I look at a loved one and not feel God's love? How can I watch a baby and doubt this love? How can I watch people's courage in the face of adversity and their hope in the face of death, and yet doubt God's love? How can I watch the sun set over the ocean, or a doe with her fawn, or hear the breeze in the trees—and doubt God's love?

What a grace: to be lost and found in God! Each day is graced with moments in which God draws us closer. God wants only that we continually live into the love that is available to us. In prayer we become aware of God's awareness of us. We pray to fall in love with God, to be consumed by God's love, to be lost in the beloved, to be found in God. We think of such things as the Lord's story of the prodigal child; and we pray for the grace to embrace God's unconditional love, to open our hearts to what God wishes to give us, and to say, unreservedly, "Yes!".

Reflection:
1) How has your experience of God's love influenced your care for others?
2) What is your image of God?
3) Has your experience of being loved by God changed that image?
4) Using the scriptures given above, pray to embrace God's unconditional love.

Activities: Surround yourself with your favorite pictures and books, spend time with your pet or in nature, see a good movie on the development of love and friendship, read some passionate love stories of Jesus, watch the sun rise or set: anything that will open your heart anew to the beauty and power of love.

Grace Received: You prayed for the grace to embrace God's unconditional love. What grace did you receive?

Such a local community,
centered in the Eucharist,
offers a concrete experience of unity in love and action.
In fact,
each of our communities is

a gathering of the people in Christ,
a cell of his mystical body.
Our common commitment,
our common way of life,
and our recognition and love of Mary as our mother
bind us together.

—General Principles, #7
(See below, p. 119.)

Twenty-Five: Spiritual Freedom

With the help of the scriptures given below, pray for the grace to become free to be Jesus's disciple.
- *Ps. 139:1-18 (created for freedom)*
- *Rom. 8:14-17 (the Spirit leads us)*
- *Lk. 15:11-32 (the prodigal son)*
- *Jn. 8:31-36 (truth will set you free).*

Spiritual freedom is the condition for and fruit of spiritual growth. It is one of the key experiences of the spiritual life. The entire spiritual journey is the growing experience of inner freedom and complete openness to God's presence. Inner freedom is a part of every stage of the spiritual journey.

Those who need to control, who need to have certainty and security in life, whose lives are defined by structure will have great difficulty in prayer. Those controlled by fear and anger, those who are dominated by the need to please or who have a fixed idea of life will be incapable of more than superficial prayer. Inner freedom is the experience of not controlling or being controlled. Becoming open to one's own desires and hopes opens one to true prayer. Freedom develops a prayer that is non-conformist, one that does not depend on the habits and expectations of others. Inner freedom is the opening to a deep and intimate relationship with God.

The word "freedom" is attractive, even compelling. Even so, there is a resistance within us to it. There seems to be a natural reluctance to allow ourselves to stand face to face with God. Handing over our lives to God rather than keeping the control ourselves is a fearsome thing. We desire freedom and at the same time resist it. We often seize the first opportunity to become dependent: "What am I supposed to get out of this prayer?"

We also avoid the risk of inner freedom by looking for methods of praying to save us: "I don't know how to pray ...

if I could just learn to do that kind of prayer . . . ." The free God wants to initiate and develop a relationship with a free human person. Staying in continuous dialogue with God helps us to understand that God desires our freedom even more than we do. Opening ourselves to what God desires for us is the move towards greater personal freedom and peace. Spiritual freedom is the opening up of ourselves to the world and to God.

Freedom helps us to be present to others, to see our lives as in service. Freedom gives us the ability to make good decisions, to build up God's Reign of Love. Freedom gives us the flexibility to move from one way of serving to another, all according to how God calls us and according to the greater need. Freedom allows us to integrate life and prayer and to find God in all things.

Spiritual freedom, then, is: *FREEDOM FROM:* enslavement to self, control of life, and paralysis from fear and anger; *FREEDOM FOR:* a life of service and intimacy with God.[*]

But more can and should be said about spiritual freedom. For several centuries before Vatican Council II, the insight (noted at the beginning of this exercise) that spiritual freedom is the condition for spiritual growth was often lost. Indeed, an opposite view held sway: feelings are suspect and are not to be trusted; one's spiritual ideals are measured by obedience to church authority.

Now, there is a need for and beauty in obedience to the church. But the depth of this response is directly related to the inner freedom with which it is offered.

Spiritual freedom is now seen for the grace it is, which is what Saint Ignatius realized five hundred years ago. It is the

---

[*] See Carolyn Osiek, RSCJ, "The First Week of the Spiritual Exercises and the Conversion of Saint Paul," in *Notes on the Spiritual Exercises of Saint Ignatius of Loyola* (St. Louis: Review for Religious, 1985), p. 87. Also see the *Canadian Manual*, p. R105.

gift of moving beyond one's fears, addictions, and compulsions, and the fruit of having a familiar and loving relationship with God. Spiritual freedom is the opening up to all creation. How attractive this is: to be so open and in touch with God that all personal blocks and barriers become surmountable!

On the other hand, spiritual freedom has its consequences. It is not concerned with doing or having only what I want. On the contrary, spiritual freedom often means receiving the inner strength to accept what I don't want. Who, for instance, looks forward to receiving the grace of not being destroyed by fear or failure? No one wants to face that. But the gift of spiritual freedom comes when I am able, through keeping my eyes on God, to accept and move beyond fear and failure when they come. For instance, facing down one's angers and despair about disease leads to acceptance and peace. Moving through one's resistance to a religious vocation opens one up to the peace and joy of mystery. And working through one's doubts and disillusionments about life issues forth into the joy and fulfillment of faith.

As is clear, spiritual freedom comes with a price; it arises out of struggle. Like Jacob, wrestling all night with the angel, we experience our spiritual freedom as the fruit of facing life with integrity and fidelity. We come to see what is true in contrast to what is false; we experience what will last, as opposed to what will fail; we embrace what is of God and turn away from what is not. From the depths of our hearts, we are increasingly able to cry out, "We are free at last!"

Reflection:
1) Is your search for God deepening your inner freedom?
2) How strong is your desire to be free?
3) What are your resistances to it?
4) Using the scriptures given above, pray to become Jesus's disciple-companion.

Ritual Activity: Watch a performance of ballet, of some dance, of some sport or other activity which expresses the freedom that we desire to have with God. Do your own gesture, movement, or dance that expresses the gift of such a free loving relationship.

Grace Received: How has God touched you? How have you been graced during these two weeks?

Twenty-Six: Being Loved Just As We Are

With the help of the following scriptures, pray for the grace to know God's love for you even in your darkest times.
- *Is. 43:1-5 (you are precious to me)*
- *Ez. 36:25-32 (I will give you a new heart)*
- *Lk. 7:36-50 (our sins are forgiven)*
- *Lk 15 (God loves sinners)*
- *2 Cor. 12:8-9 (my grace is enough for you).*

Imagine being totally forgiven by one you love but have hurt deeply. The regret, confusion, sadness, and embarrassment bite deep, and you dread coming face to face again with this friend. Of course it happens, and you are received with forgiveness and acceptance. All of your attempts to explain and apologize are waved aside, and the reunion is simply the rejoicing in being together again. It is the story of the prodigal child: no excuses or explanations are wanted, not even apologies. It is simply the total love and joy at having the child back. Such an experience would be overwhelming, never forgotten; and the child would be forever changed.

Even more telling is the example of a mother the author knew who forgave her son-in-law for taking the life of her daughter. She wrote him in prison, "Don't let this ruin your life. You are a young man. I know you didn't mean it; you must have been very angry." This epitomizes the forgiving love of Jesus.

These are metaphors of God's love for us in our worst times. That love seems unreal, too good to be true. But that love is what we are asked to believe in this exercise, and we will begin to get a glimpse of what this means only when we have once experienced ourselves forgiven and accepted back unconditionally for our stance of utter indifference and rejection. Fortunately, this is our God. We do not have to comprehend it. We need merely to accept it.

To be embraced by God and know such unconditional love is a powerful experience. It almost seems overwhelming, especially when we feel vulnerable and weak, especially when we have not been loving ourselves. It leads us to want to respond to God with our own hearts filled with love.

With Paul, however, we must sometimes say, "That which we desire we do not do, and that which we do not desire we do" (Rom. 7:15). Within us is the desire to respond to God. Also within us is a desire to hold that love back, to do things our own way. Whenever we make ourselves or any part of God's creation central in our lives, or whenever we tolerate structures in society that deprive others of their dignity and freedom, we become unbalanced in our relationship with God. This is the biblical notion of sin.

And yet even in this, God continues to love us. In fact, it is only in experiencing God's love that we are able to recognize our lack of love. Sin is a subtle thing. Just as the light reveals the shadows, sin must be revealed to us; we are blind to our own darkness. We can recognize our lack of love only after having first experienced being loved, and unless we have known love, we will not recognize when it is absent. It is God who reveals our dark side to us through loving us. The point of emphasis is not on how much we are sinners but on how much we are loved. The good news of the Gospel is that even though we do not deserve it, God totally loves us anyway, just as we are. We cannot escape this or hide from it.

There is a paradox here. By our descending with God's loving power into our own deaths, wounds, alienation, sadness, fear, and self-hatred, there arise new inspirations, healing, and life. The point where these two currents cross is the greatest pain. It is, in the terminology of addiction, "hitting bottom." But it is out of this conflict that pain is transformed into the energy to begin anew. The cycle of death and rebirth is once again lived out, and we learn with the help of God's loving grace that in embracing our brokenness, we discover our freedom and strength.

Our failures need not be our enemies, nor need our failures control us; they can in faith become points of grace. It is in our weakness that God's strength and forgiving love are revealed. It is in our worst times that we can most clearly see how true it is what Paul says when he writes to the Corinthians, "My grace is enough for you, for in weakness power reaches perfection. And so I willingly boast of my weaknesses instead, that the power of Christ may rest on me" (2 Cor. 12:9). The resurrection happens on Calvary. We need no longer be afraid; we know in a new way what it means to be saved. God's unconditional love is once again made manifest.*

Reflection:
1) How has the incredible mystery of God's love for you been revealed in your reaching out to others?
2) Where in your life are you not loving? Do you play a part in the sins of society?
3) Does your experience of sin bring you to hopelessness or to faith?
4) Using the scriptures above, pray for the grace to know God's love for you even in your times of darkness.

Activity: Do a mantra—a word or short phrase that is repeated frequently as a prayer—"Spirit," or "Jesus, have mercy on me," or a word or phrase of your own choosing.

Grace Received: Did you receive the grace you prayed for in this exercise? What grace did you receive?

---

* See Carolyn Osiek, RSCJ, "The First Week of the Spiritual Exercises and the Conversion of Saint Paul," *Notes on the Spiritual Exercises of Saint Ignatius of Loyola, op. cit.,* p. 87. See also the *Canadian Manual,* p. R105.

Twenty-Seven: Intimate Union with Christ

With the help of the scriptures given on p. 101 of this exercise, pray to understand and desire for yourself Jesus's way of life.

Having an intimate relationship with Christ is an invitation and a challenge. We normally do not think of him or relate to him in a context like this. Rather, He seems remote and out of reach. A passage from the sixth general principle of CLC makes this invitation to intimate union seem more possible:

Union with Christ leads to union with the Church where Christ here and now continues his mission of salvation. By making ourselves sensitive to the signs of the times and the movements of the Spirit, we will be better able to encounter Christ in all persons and in all situations [General Principles, #6; see below, p. 118f].

Christ is more than someone who lived "back then"; he is one who is living right now in our midst. To encounter Christ is not to bridge a span of 2000 years; it is to reach out to him in the person next to us, in the situations in which we find ourselves. Christ reveals himself through others and in turn reveals others to us. When we see and love someone, we see and love Christ. When we watch and come to love Jesus in the Gospel, we come to love the others around us. This is a circle, and its deepening spiral continually draws us more profoundly into this truth until our love for Christ and our love for one another are the same. This is real, this is flesh and blood, this is intimate, this is Eucharist, this is finding God in all things.

As Jesus takes on more reality, we find him more daunting and challenging than we anticipated. For instance, he may call us in ways that we resist, or to a ministry that asks much from us; or he may not invite us into a particular ministry that we would like. It may be that he will accept our prayer to be with him in his passion. Or it may be that his resurrection calls us to forgive when we are not ready to do so. The grace of developing an adult relationship with Jesus will be that these situations will not jeopardize our love for him.

Loving Jesus intimately may seem too much to hope for. "Intimate" can involve intense feelings. It is a deep acceptance of Jesus as brother and savior. Our feelings also may not be intense; in fact, they may seem rather bland and vapid. That is all right; our intimate union with him does not depend on how strongly we may feel at any one time. It is our unreserved trust in and commitment to him that bears out our union with him. Even the desire to be this united with Jesus indicates the truth that in fact we already are. It is in our ongoing, up-and-down life experiences that our oneness with Jesus is exercised, and our encounter of love for him is made more real.

We can know Jesus intimately only when he reveals himself to us. We pray for this grace, and we contemplate him in the Gospel stories so as to come to know him. The Gospels are privileged writings through which he reveals himself. The scripture passages that follow may be helpful in coming to know him.

- *Mk. 8:29 (Jesus asks us: "And you: who do you say that I am?")*
- *Mt. 5:3ff. (beatitudes)*
- *Mt. 5:24 (leave your gift at the altar, and go first and be reconciled with your brother or sister)*
- *Mt. 5:44 (love your enemies)*
- *Mt. 6:14 (if you forgive others, your Father in heaven will forgive you)*
- *Jn. 13:14 (if I have washed your feet, you must wash one another's feet)*
- *Lk 18:16 (let the children come to me)*
- *Lk. 23:34 (Father, forgive them, for they do not know what they are doing)*
- *Jn. 20:16 (Mary!)*
- *1 Cor. 13 (love is patient, love is kind. . . .)*

Prayer:

♦ Ask Mary to intercede for you to become detached from all things and to put all your talents, possessions, and achievements at the service of Christ. Pray to follow in the pattern of Christ, even to the end. Pray that if it is God's wish for you, you would have, like Christ, the courage and strength to endure poverty and personal humiliation for love of him. Pray the *Hail Mary*.

♦ In the company of Mary, ask Jesus to obtain this grace for you from his Father. Then pray the *Soul of Christ* prayer, given above on page xvii in the Foreword.

♦ In the presence of Mary and Jesus, and with your prayer being offered by them, approach Jesus's Father, making the same request for the grace to be totally united with Christ. Pray the *Our Father.**

Reflection:

1) How have your love for others and your love of Christ impacted each other?

2) Is Christ manifest in your life? Which of your feelings and attitudes are Christ-like, and which are not?

3) How have you experienced Jesus freeing you from the power of death?

4) Using the scriptures that have been given in this chapter, pray to understand and desire for yourself the way of life of Jesus.

---

* See "On Asking God to Reveal Himself in Retreat," in *Notes on the Spiritual Exercises of Saint Ignatius of Loyola, op. cit.,* p. 76.

Symbol: Find two symbols: one expressing your relationship with Jesus as it is now, and one expressing the relationship you desire to have with him. Place them together, and let these differing relationships with him become one.

Grace Received: What is the grace you received during this time? Is it challenging? frightening? comforting?

Twenty-Eight: Community Reflection on the Unconditional Love of God

With the help of the following scriptures, pray for the grace to know and love Jesus more, that you may share in his mission of salvation.

- *Dt. 7:7-9 (the Lord set his heart on you)*
- *Is. 54:5-10 (my love shall never leave you)*
- *Hos. 11:1-11 (when Israel was a child)*
- *Jer. 29:11-15 (I have plans in mind for you)*
- *Eph. 1:3-6 (every blessing is in Christ).*

Meetings 24 through 27 had to do with God's loving us: God's Unconditional Love, Spiritual Freedom, Being Loved Just As We Are, and Intimate Union with Christ. As you come to the end of Volume I of the "Exercises for Spiritual Growth in Christian Life Community," it would be good to reflect, both as individuals and as a community, on your life and growth since beginning CLC.

The following questions may be helpful for this.

- ◆ How have I experienced God's presence during this time?
- ◆ What exercises from this unit on God's loving us struck me particularly?
- ◆ How has this experience affected me:
  - • in my service to others?
  - • in my desire to know and follow Christ more?
  - • in my commitment to those around me, to this community?
- ◆ What growth have I seen in this group? In its striving to live out the mission of Christ?
- ◆ Where is this community being called in its growth and in its ministry?
- ◆ What issues do I feel need to be addressed by this community?
- ◆ Anything else?

Reflection:
  1) How have your experience of these past four exercises and your work for the well-being of others influenced each other?
  2) You might consider doing a ritual for this meeting to celebrate the community's life and service, ending with a party/social of some kind.
  3) It may be good for the community to spend a day or weekend in prayer and discernment regarding its future direction.
  4) Using the scriptures given above, pray for the grace to discern God's call for this community.

Ritual: Use movements with formal prayer to help reveal your deepest desires, which are God's desires for you.

Grace Received: What graces have you received during the span of these past four exercises? Are they the graces you prayed for? How are they different? What is this saying to you?

Because our Community is a way of Christian life,
these principles are to be interpreted
not so much by the letter of this text
as by the spirit of the Gospel and the interior law of love.
This law of love,
which the Spirit inscribes in our hearts,
expresses itself anew in each situation of our daily lives.
This Spirit-inspired love
respects the uniqueness of each personal vocation
and enables us to be open and free,

always at the disposal of God.
It challenges us to see our responsibilities
and constantly to see answers to the needs of our times,
to work together with the entire people of God
and all people of good will
to seek progress and peace,
justice and charity,
liberty and dignity
for all.

—General Principles, #2
(See below, page 117.)

Appendices

Appendix I: Leading a Community in Prayer
Sylvia A. Swanke, RSM[*]

The following ideas and suggestions have come about from the requests of many CLC members who feel the need for some assistance in leading prayer for their meetings. What follow are offered as samples of what can be done; they have been used by the author and others, but by no means ought to be viewed as the only way of leading a community in prayer. If these suggestions are helpful, then please use them in your meetings. At the end of this article you will find a category called "Creative Possibilities." I have the feeling that most of the people in CLC have experienced many creative ways of praying. My hope is that, after using some of the suggestions here, you will reach into your own soul and devise your own ways of leading the group in prayer.

A word about prayer, first. It is not something we do. It is a way of being. It is an opening of ourselves to allow God to be with us. Now, God is with us always; but we don't always recognize this reality. We bring ourselves to prayer to bring ourselves to the awareness of God. Some have said that prayer is a way of opening ourselves so that God can pray in us. In CLC we quickly learn that all we do is of God, and so prayer is a continual opening to allow God to be known to us. In eastern religions, prayer is considered the means to assist us to be "awake" so as to come to know the divine within. Whatever we consider prayer to be, it is a part of the whole of our lives.

The following are some possibilities for leading a community in prayer.

---

[*] It was largely through Sr. Sylvia's efforts that CLC had its beginnings in the northwestern United States in 1988. — LGsj.

Music:

The use of music can be very helpful in setting a tone for quiet and prayerfulness. If a prayer is to be read, some background music is helpful. Instrumental music works best for this. Much classical and new age music is instrumental and good for quieting. Contemporary church music today also offers a reflective tone, with the words being scripturally based. It is also good at times to sing a song together. There is no one fixed norm about the kind of music to use in a meeting. The rule of thumb would be, "How can this music help move the group to a quiet, reflective place?" At the end of these suggestions will be found a listing of some tapes of music that may be useful in leading prayer.

Readings and Prayers:

Just a word on the spoken word. Whether a person is reading a section from an article or book or is reading a prayer, care must be taken that the reading is done in a helpful way. The reader would do well to read slowly and reflectively, so as to allow those listening to be able to reflect as the reading is done. When the reader is finished, time could then to given to silent reflection on the reading.

Silence:

Taking a time of quiet and silence can often assist a person to move into a reflective state. Very often after the check-in at the meetings, it is helpful to move the group to silence as a way of coming from all the noise and activity of the day. Silence can be coupled with some relaxation methods which then provide a time of quiet. Silence can also be a way to close the faith sharing.

Relaxation Methods:

One relaxation method is to guide the group through a process of bodily awareness. This method is used in Anthony deMello's book *Sadhana: a Way to God*. By becoming aware of our body, we also become aware of the Spirit within. There are many ways of doing these exercises. The following is one way.

Get in a comfortable position, feet on the floor, back against the chair, arms relaxed. (Pause.) Close your eyes and become aware of the sounds around you. Simply listen to them; don't try to figure them out—just listen. Now let them go. (Pause.) Now become aware of your body. (Pause). Feel your feet on the floor (pause); be aware of your legs: how they are positioned, if they feel tense. (Pause.) Feel your buttocks against the chair. (Pause.) Be aware of your back; feel it against the chair. (Pause.) Feel your arms and your shoulders; allow the weight you carry on your shoulders to be lifted and allow yourself to feel lighter. (Pause.) Move your awareness up toward your head. Become aware of your thoughts, the movements in your mind. Begin to let these thoughts go. Image your head as having an opening at the top and allow all that is going on in it simply to drift out. Be aware, be aware of what you are feeling and simply allow yourself to be in that feeling. (Pause, and allow a few minutes of quiet.) Begin now to return, to come into this room, to become aware of being with this community. When you are ready, open your eyes and be present here in this room.

Scripture:

The use of scripture is also a way to lead the group into reflection and quiet before the faith sharing. Often one of the scriptures suggested on the exercise sheet is good to use to move people into the theme for the sharing. Use of the psalms can be helpful to assist in developing a reflective spirit. The psalms often have nature images in them which can move one to be in the heart rather than in the head. Being in the heart leads to speaking from the heart in the faith sharing. In using the psalms, it is good to read slowly from just a few verses rather than reading a lengthy section or an entire passage. A psalm can also be used to close faith sharing or at the end of the meeting.

Formal Prayer:
Formal prayers may be used at any or all of the places where prayer is called for: at the beginning of the meeting, when closing the faith sharing, or when concluding the meeting. Saint Ignatius often suggests the use of the *Our Father* to close meditations. The *Hail Mary, Glory Be*, or any other known formal prayers may be suitable.

Prayers of Petition:
Very often we know of people who have asked for or need our prayers. It would be appropriate to use the prayer of petition at CLC gatherings, as this connects us to all in the Body of Christ. Two times that prayers of petition might be used would be at the close of the faith sharing or at the end of a meeting. In either case this type of prayer widens the circle of our lives and includes those who need or have requested prayers from us.

Gesture:
Prayer does not always have to be something we read or listen to. It does not have to be done sitting. Gesture, movement, even without words, can be a powerful prayer. Gestures can be done to the Our Father, to many of the contemporary church songs, or even to a single stanza of a poem.

Use of Symbol:
Sometimes using an object to evoke symbolic awareness can lead to a reflective mood. The object used can be something from nature, an abstract picture, a candle, or any other object that may evoke symbolic feelings. The following are some ways to use symbols:

A Rock: A rock is placed on a table in the center of the group. The group is asked to contemplate the rock for a few minutes. After a time of silent reflection, each person, or those who wish, may say what the rock symbolizes for them this evening. This may also be done by passing the rock from person to person. Some responses might be: "At times I feel a hardness within me, and I want to remove this hardness so as to be pliable with God." Or, "This rock is smooth from being worn down by water, and it symbolizes that for me my baptism with water is an agreement to be run over continually with the love of God and to be worn down to God's desires." Symbolic expressions may include pain, joy, mystery, reconciliation, and any number of things. The point of these exercises is to move us into the heart so that we may then be able to express the reflections we have had during the time since our last gathering.

Flowers: This was used by one person leading prayer. The prayer leader brought small branches from a flowering tree. There was a branch for each person. Each was given one and asked to contemplate it for a few minutes. Then each person was asked to say what the flowering, what the spring, or what in general this branch represented to him or her. They were asked to relate this symbolic object to the new life of spring. As each spoke of his or her ponderings, the branch was placed in a vase in the center of the group. The vase was then left in the middle of the group during the faith sharing as its own symbol of the union of the group.

Personal Symbols: before the meeting, the prayer leader may ask each person to bring to the meeting a symbol that has had particular meaning to him or her. These symbols may represent a healing that has been experienced, or a friendship that has been developed, or a loss that has been known, or the birth of a child, or the death of a parent, or the release of a burden. The same process as above is used to relate the symbolic meaning to each person's object. After each person shares his or her symbol, it could be placed on a table in the center of the group and left there until the end of the sharing.

Creative Possibilities:

Once you have used some of the suggestions given in these pages, you may want to begin creating your own methods for leading the group in prayer. Do it! Begin to create your own meditative forms and prayers; begin to share these with your CLC community, using gestures, candles, slides, or whatever symbol or method you may choose.

Some Aids in Leading a Community in Prayer:
  Books:

DeMello, Anthony, *Sadhana: A Way to God* (St. Louis: Institute of Jesuit Sources, 1978)

------, *Song of the Bird* (New York: Doubleday and Co., Inc., 1984)

Hays, Edward M., *Prayers for a Planetary Pilgrim* (Easton, KS: Forest Peace Books, Inc., 1989)

Leadingham, Carrie; Moschella, Joann; Varatanian, Hilary M., *Peace Prayers* (San Francisco: Harper, 1992)

Loder, Ted, *Guerillas of Grace* (San Diego: Lura Media, 1984)

Roberts, Elizabeth; Amidon, Elias (eds)., *Earth Prayers* (San Francisco: Harper, 1991)

Schrenk, Nancy, OSF; Leach, Maureen, OSF, *Psalms Anew* (Winona, MN: St. Mary's Press, 1986).

Music: Classical Instrumental

J.S. Bach, "Air in G"

Samuel Barber, "Adagio for Strings," from the string quartet, op. 11.

L. von Beethoven, "Moonlight Sonata"

Giovanni Pergolesi, excerpts from "Stabat Mater"

Sergei Rachmaninoff, "Vespers"

Antonio Vivaldi, adagio, from the concerto in d minor for guitar

Antonio Vivaldi, "The Four Seasons," specifically "Winter"

Music: Contemporary Instrumental

"Fairy Ring"

Theme from the movie "Mission"

"Somewhere in Time"

Theme from the movie "Chariots of Fire"

Music of Kitaro

Georgia Kelly, "Seapeace"

Chants and flute music from native Americans

Music by Zamfir

Zen music

Meditation music

Brian Eno, "Ambient 1, Music for Airports"

Music: Contemporary Hymns and Songs

Saint Louis Jesuits

Monks of Weston Priory

Community of Taize

David Haas

Marty Haugen

Bob Hurd

Michael Toncas

Suzanne Toolan

Appendix II: Bibliography

Office of English Canada Christian Life Community, *English Canadian Formation Manual I* (Guelph, Ontario, 1989). The themes outlined and the resources articles provided in this manual were of great assistance in helping develop the present book.

David L. Fleming, S.J., (ed.), *Notes on the Spiritual Exercises of Saint Ignatius of Loyola* (St. Louis: Review for Religious. 1985). There is a wealth of wisdom and insight into the Spiritual Exercises of St. Ignatius in this book. Particularly helpful were those on the various aspects of the first and second weeks.

Marian Cowan, C.S.J., and John Carroll Futrell, S.J., *The Spiritual Exercises of St. Ignatius of Loyola: a Handbook for Directors* (New York: Le Jacq Publication Company, 1982). This book offers a uniquely precise analysis of the Spiritual Exercises that the author of this manual has referred to again and again.

Henri Nouwen, *The Way of the Heart: a Desert Spirituality* (New York: Seabury Press, 1981).

Adrien Demoustier, S.J., and Jean-Yves Calvez, S.J., "The Disturbing Subject: the Option for the Poor," *Studies in the Spirituality of Jesuits* (Saint Louis: Seminar on Jesuit Spirituality, XXI, 2 [March, 1989]).

Christian Life Community of the U.S., *General Principles and General Norms),* July, 1992.

Appendix III

Excerpts from the General Principles and General norms of CLC
(Approved U.S.A. Version, July, 1992.)

A. General Principles
1. *Response to God's Love:*
Out of love, the Word became human and was born of Mary. . . . Jesus invites all of us, in living with the poor and sharing their condition, to give ourselves continuously to God and to bring about unity in our human family. Inspired by the Holy Spirit, we respond with gratitude to God for this gift of Jesus in every circumstance in our lives.

2. *Guided by the Spirit:*
Because our community is a way of Christian life, these principles are to be interpreted not so much by the letter of this text as by the spirit of the Gospel and the interior law of love. This law of love, which the Spirit inscribes in our hearts, expresses itself anew in each situation of our daily lives. This Spirit-inspired love respects the uniqueness of each personal vocation and enables us to be open and free, always at the disposal of God. It challenges us to see our responsibilities and constantly to seek answers to the needs of our times, to work together with the entire people of God and all people of good will to seek progress and peace, justice and charity, liberty and dignity for all.

3. *Graced History:*
We live this way of Christian life in joyful communion with all those who have preceded us, grateful for their efforts and apostolic accomplishments. In love and prayer we join those many men and women of our spiritual tradition who have

been proposed to us by the Church as friends and valid intercessors who help us fulfill our mission.

4. *Missioned Communities:*

We propose to commit ourselves as Christians in bearing witness to those human and Gospel values within the Church and society which affect the dignity of the person, the welfare of the family, and the integrity of creation. We are especially aware of the pressing need to work for justice through a preferential option for the poor and a simple lifestyle which expresses our freedom and solidarity with them.

5. *Discerning Communities:*

We hold the Spiritual Exercises of Saint Ignatius as the specific source and the characteristic instrument of our spirituality. Our vocation calls us to live this spirituality, which opens and disposes us to whatever God wishes in each concrete situation of our daily life. We recognize particularly the necessity of prayer and discernment, personal and communal, of the daily examination of consciousness and of spiritual guidance as important means for seeking and finding God in all things.

6. *Sense of Church:*

Union with Christ leads to union with the Church, where Christ here and now continues his mission of salvation. By making ourselves sensitive to the signs of the times and movements of the Spirit, we will be better able to encounter Christ in all persons and in all situations. Sharing the riches of membership in the Church, we participate in the liturgy, meditate upon the scriptures, and learn, teach, and promote Christian doctrine. We work together with the hierarchy and other ecclesial leaders, motivated by common concern for the problems and progress of all people and open to the situations in which the Church finds itself today. This sense of the Church impels us to creative and concrete collaboration for the work of advancing the reign of God on earth, and includes a readiness to go and serve where the needs of the Church so demand.

7. Creative Community:

We express the giving of ourselves by personal commitment to the world community, through a freely chosen local community. Such a local community, centered in the Eucharist, offers a concrete experience of unity in love and action. In fact, each of our communities is a gathering of the people in Christ, a cell of his mystical body. Our common commitment, our common way of life, and our recognition and love of Mary as our mother bind us together. Our responsibility to develop the bonds of community does not stop with our local community but extends to the national and world Christian Life Community, to the ecclesial communities of which we are part (parish, diocese), to the whole Church, and to all people of good will.

8. Apostolic Life:

Christ has sent us on mission as members of the pilgrim people of God to be his witnesses before all people by our attitudes, words, and actions. We are to become identified with his mission of bringing the good news to the poor, proclaiming liberty to captives and to the blind, new sight, setting the downtrodden free and proclaiming the Lord's year of favor. Our life is essentially apostolic. The field of CLC mission knows no limits: it extends both to the Church and the world, in order to bring the Gospel of salvation to all people and to serve individual persons and society by opening hearts to conversion and struggling to change oppressive structures.

9. Union with Mary:

Since the spirituality of our community is centered on Christ, we see the role of Mary in relation to Christ. She is the model of our own collaboration in Christ's mission. Mary's co-operation with God begins with her "yes" in the mystery of the Annunciation-Incarnation. Her effective service, as shown in her visit to Elizabeth, makes her our inspiration to act for justice in the world today.

B. General Norms:

12a. Way of Life:

The way of life of Christian Life Community commits its members, with the help of the community, to strive for continuing personal and social growth which is spiritual, human, and apostolic. In practice, this involves participating in the Eucharist whenever possible, an active sacramental life, daily practice of personal prayer (especially that based on sacred scripture), discernment by means of daily review of one's life (and, if possible, regular spiritual direction), an annual interior renewal in accordance with the sources of our spirituality, and a love for the Mother of God.

Appendix IV

Twenty-Nine: Looking Back
As We Look Ahead: An Exercise
During Times of Transition

With the help of the following scripture passages, pray for the grace to grow in intimacy with God.
- *Song of Songs, 2:10: (come, my lovely one)*
- *1 Sam 3:1-10 (speak, your servant is listening)*
- *Is. 55:1-6 (God loves me)*
- *Jer. 29:11-15 (I have plans for you)*
- *Lk. 15:11-32 (prodigal child).*

When we open ourselves to grow spiritually, perspectives change. For one thing, we realize more clearly that prayer is a matter of relationship. Intimacy is the basic issue, not resolutions "to be better" or answers to problems. Many problems and challenges have no answers, but they can be faced and lived through with more peace and resilience if we know we are not alone. Pain is more bearable when we have poured out our sorrows and anger to God and have experienced God's intimate presence to us. Will power alone cannot achieve what we want. What we desire is a gift which only God can give.

Freedom is at the heart of the process. No one, neither God nor ourselves, can be forced into intimacy. God freely gives Self to us in God's own way. We are all promised the grace of salvation, but not all the graces we desire may be given to us, such as the desire to enter into Jesus's own suffering or the grace of a specific ministry or vocation in life. Our freedom is to be open to God's own way with us without trying to coerce

God into our framework of seeing and doing. God wants not petulant demands or dumb submission, but rather spontaneous love.

Our relationship with God tends to take on a more adult flavor when we look on prayer in this interpersonal way. We come to realize that we are not asking for graces much as a child asks for candy, but for intimacy which requires relative maturity on our parts.

You are about to begin a new phase in CLC. You will be meeting the same God again that you met in the past. It is the same God inviting you to come closer as the "beloved, the lovely one." God desires intimacy with you. God desires to share life with you. As you look back and remember how God has been within you and your community, you will be opening yourselves up to see how God is wanting to be with you in the future.*

Reflection:
1) How did your living for others and your experience of this past phase of CLC influence each other?
2) Looking ahead, what deep hopes and longings do you have regarding your relationship with God and with this community? What are your fears and obstacles?
3) Using the scriptures given above or those of your own choice, pray for the grace to receive in freedom and trust God's intimate loving care for you.
4) Next meeting's faith sharing will come out of your experience of this exercise.

---

* For more on this, see William A. Barry, S.J., "On Asking God to Reveal Himself in Retreat," *Notes on the Spiritual Exercises of St. Ignatius of Loyola, op. cit.,* pp.72-77.

Ritual Activity: Find a flower or a piece of art that symbolizes the graces you received during the past phase of your CLC experience. Spend time with it frequently during the next two weeks.

Grace Received: In what way did you grow spiritually and as a member of the CLC community during this time? How were you graced by God?

God's Grandeur

The world is charged with the grandeur of God.
It will flame out, like shining from shook foil;
It gathers to a greatness, like the ooze of oil
Crushed. Why do men then now not reck his rod?
Generations have trod, have trod, have trod;
And all is seared with trade; bleared, smeared with toil;
And wears man's smudge and shares man's smell: the soil
Is bare now, nor can foot feel, being shod.

And for all this, nature is never spent;
There lives the dearest freshness deep down things;
And though the last lights off the black West went
Oh, morning, at the brown brink eastward, springs—
Because the Holy Ghost over the bent
World broods with warm breast and with ah! bright wings.

Gerard Manley Hopkins, S.J.